The Future of Arms Control

The Future of Arms Control

Michael A. Levi

Michael E. O'Hanlon

BROOKINGS INSTITUTION PRESS
Washington, D.C.

1775 Massachusetts Avenue, N.W., Washington, D.C. 20036
www.brookings.edu

Library of Congress Cataloging-in-Publication data

Levi, Michael A.
The future of arms control / Michael A. Levi, Michael E. O'Hanlon.
p. cm.
Summary: "Lays out the framework of an enduring and effective arms control strategy that is explicitly linked to broader U.S. security policy, focusing on preventing the spread of nuclear and biological arms to extremist states and terrorist organizations"—Provided by publisher.
Includes bibliographical references and index.
ISBN 0-8157-6462-6 (cloth : alk. paper) —
ISBN 0-8157-6463-4 (pbk. : alk. paper)
1. Arms control—United States. 2. United States—Foreign relations. 3. International relations. 4. Security, International. 5. Nuclear disarmament. I. O'Hanlon, Michael E. II. Title.
JZ5687.L48 2005
327.1'74—dc22 2004021714

9 8 7 6 5 4 3 2 1

The paper used in this publication meets minimum requirements of the American National Standard for Information Sciences—Permanence of Paper for Printed Library Materials: ANSI Z39.48-1992.

Typeset in Sabon

Composition by R. Lynn Rivenbark
Macon, Georgia

Printed by R. R. Donnelley
Harrisonburg, Virginia

FROM MICHAEL LEVI

TO MY GRANDPARENTS

AND

FROM MICHAEL O'HANLON

TO AUNT PAT AND JOE

Contents

Foreword

Today, even the phrase "arms control" has a somewhat musty quality. SALT, START, IMF, CFE—all those initials and acronyms remind us of the days when the American and Soviet diplomats squared off across negotiating tables in Geneva and Helsinki to haggle over warheads, throw-weight, launchers, armored personnel carriers, and the numerology of Armageddon. The specifics often were a subject of controversy, not just between the superpowers but within the Western strategic community. But guided by common sense, pragmatism, and the demands of traditional diplomacy, most practitioners of American foreign policy—on the left and on the right—recognized the broad importance of arms control as a necessary means of keeping the cold war from turning hot. The objectives articulated by Thomas Schelling and Morton Halperin (who later became a Brookings senior fellow) in the early 1960s—reducing the costs of preparing for war, the chances of war, and the damage that would result from any war that did occur—were recognized as compelling. Mercifully, the third objective was never tested, and most would agree that arms control made a contribution on the first two.

Dwight Eisenhower's Atoms for Peace plan led to the Johnson administration's successful efforts to help negotiate the Nuclear Non-Proliferation Treaty; John Kennedy pushed for limits on nuclear testing with bipartisan support in the Congress; Richard Nixon's detente efforts with the Soviet Union had the SALT and ABM accords on offensive and defensive nuclear arms as a centerpiece; and various communications and "hotline" agreements were reached during the Nixon administration. Finally, while he began his presidency as a critic of much previous arms control, Ronald Reagan wound up working with Soviet premier Mikhail Gorbachev to achieve some of the most dramatic arms limitation breakthroughs of the cold war, in a process that played out into the first Bush presidency and the early years of the Clinton administration.

But once the cold war ended, the consensus that had undergirded arms control for so long began to crumble. The danger against which arms control purportedly offered protection was now more diffuse and inchoate; the importance of formal accords was no longer so obvious; the earlier need to restrain an all-out competition between two rival superpowers was now in the dustbin of history. The presidency of George W. Bush, September 11, and the administration's global war on terror only underscored these new realities and called into question whether negotiations and treaties were any longer of any use in restraining the nation's enemies.

Yet, as this book argues, arms control is hardly obsolete. While new strategic dynamics do call into question the kind of diplomacy practiced for so long in the previous era, terrorism, coupled with trends in modern technology, now underscores the need to limit the spread of biological, nuclear, and other potentially lethal materials as well as dangerous arms. If the definition of arms control is taken to be simply that—to cooperate internationally in controlling dangerous technologies and arms, without prejudging its basic methods or participants or modalities—there can be little debate about its continued necessity and desirability.

Michael Levi and Michael O'Hanlon begin with the premise that we must use all the means available, including what might be called an updated version of classic arms control, to impede the spread of weapons of mass destruction in an age of catastrophic terror (as well as other challenges). We must combine the threat and, if necessary, the use of military force with diplomacy and judicious use of arms control techniques. Those include some new ones developed by the Bush administration, such as the promising Proliferation Security Initiative, as well as approaches developed by earlier administrations, such as the emphasis that the first President Bush and President Clinton put on greatly expanding inspections to address the threat of nuclear proliferation.

The authors offer concise, concrete, and thought-provoking suggestions. They do so in a framework that stresses the need for clear priorities, most notably dealing with nuclear and biological technologies and their potential proliferation. The authors endorse some "traditional" arms control accords, such as the Comprehensive Test Ban Treaty. But they also support some Bush administration initiatives, such as the very nontraditional U.S.-Russia Strategic Offensive Reductions Treaty, as well as the administration's Proliferation Security Initiative. And they share at least some of the administration's skepticism about the verification protocol to the Biological Weapons Convention as well as the Ottawa land mines accord. They can imagine that in the new era, unlike the previous one, arms control should not be viewed merely as an alternative to war. Rather, it can sometimes serve to sound an early warning about dangerous proliferation activities, thereby establishing a predicate for coercive action up to and including the use of force in extreme cases.

In the bargain that lies at the heart of the Nuclear Non-Proliferation Treaty, the nuclear powers that are party to the treaty agree to abolish their arsenals over time, while the other parties, in exchange for that assurance and for assistance with their civil nuclear power programs, agree not to pursue nuclear weapons. Without calling for a formal change to the NPT, Mike Levi and Mike O'Hanlon suggest major changes in how that bargain should be understood. They argue that it is wrongheaded and even dangerous to help other countries gain the means to develop nuclear weapons more quickly under the guise of developing civilian programs. In particular, non-nuclear countries should not be encouraged or helped to develop their own capacity to produce or reprocess nuclear fuel, even if it is alleged to be for energy generation. That requires a change in how the NPT has been understood since its signing.

More broadly they suggest that, following the logic of NATO enlargement, the United States and its allies should offer a vision of collective security to nonaggressive countries that are moving toward democracy and playing a responsible role on the international stage. Security guarantees can be used with an increasing number of states to help them provide for their own defense without acquiring nuclear weapons. This vision will take time to implement, but it is more realistic than calls for the universal abolition of nuclear arms and more responsive to the true security needs of countries that might be tempted to acquire weapons of mass destruction in the coming years and decades.

The authors insist that while asking others for help in controlling the proliferation of nuclear and biological weapons, Western countries must also take seriously the arms issues that plague many developing countries—notably the small arms trade. Small arms are the weapons of mass destruction in much of the developing world, and a strong humanitarian rationale therefore exists for seeking to limit their use and spread. In addition, if the United States expects the help of most other countries in countering the most serious threats to its own security, it must promote an arms control strategy that responds to the needs and priorities of non-Western states as well. The small arms commerce is extremely difficult to regulate, and formal treaties have little to offer in that regard. However, undertaking a coordinated effort to tighten domestic regulation and oversight among major weapons producers can help at least somewhat, and a serious attempt should be made to do so.

It is hard to imagine a more timely attempt to deal with one of the most onerous challenges facing the nation and the world. Brookings is proud to have on its staff scholars who are up to the task, and we are grateful for the support we have received from the Carnegie Corporation of New York and the John D. and Catherine T. MacArthur Foundation in bringing this book to you.

STROBE TALBOTT
President, Brookings Institution

Washington, D.C.
September 2004

Acknowledgments

The authors are deeply grateful to Richard Betts, Richard Garwin, Jan Lodal, and Thomas Schelling for painstaking efforts to help them improve the manuscript. They further thank members of the arms control working group at Brookings during the 2002–04 period and those who gave presentations or wrote papers: Kurt Campbell, Christopher Chyba, Helle Dale, Rose Gottemoeller, Elisa Harris, Theresa Hitchens, Michael Krepon, Tod Lindberg, Jan Lodal, Georgi Mamedov, Roger Molander, David Mosher, Baker Spring, and John Steinbruner. Other participants in the working group sessions included Bruce Blair, Alexei Bogaturov, Avis Bohlen, Lael Brainard, Joe Cirincione, Lynn Davis, Tom Davis, Kim Dong-Shin, Lewis Dunn, Robert Einhorn, Lee Feinstein, Harold Feiveson, Ann Florini, Alton Frye, Nancy Gallagher, Robert Gallucci, James Goodby, Frank von Hippel, John Ikenberry, Fred Ikle, Daryl Kimball, Andy Krepinevich, Ellen Laipson, Bill Lynn, Jessica Mathews, Michael Moodie, Janne Nolan, George Perkovich, Thomas Pickering, Daniel Poneman, George Quester, Gary Schmitt, David Smith, Helmut Sonnenfeldt, Angela Stent, Victor Utgoff, and Celeste Wallander. They thank James Steinberg for reviewing several drafts, as well as Strobe Talbott and colleagues in the Brookings Foreign Policy Studies program, including Stephen Cohen, Ivo Daalder, Cliff Gaddy, Fiona Hill, James Lindsay, Susan Rice, Jeremy Shapiro, and Peter Singer. Of course, none of the individuals mentioned should be held responsible for any of the ideas that appear in this book, though the authors acknowledge a substantial intellectual debt to all of them.

CHAPTER 1

Introduction and Rationale

Arms control, for decades a key tool of American foreign policy, is nearly moribund today. Its detractors denounce it as dangerous and outmoded, while its advocates often pin high hopes on its ability to fundamentally alter the international security environment. Most Americans, meanwhile, ignore what appears to be a shrill and unimportant debate. As a result, politicians largely avoid acquiring any detailed understanding of the subject.

This combination of factors—polarized debate among specialists, indifference throughout the population at large, neglect by political leaders—is unhealthy. Arms control is still important, because dangerous technologies abound and no practical strategy exists whereby one country or small group of countries can successfully safeguard them. Coordinated international effort to regulate the development, production, and use of the world's most threatening technologies—in other words, arms control—is imperative. But the old ways of pursuing arms control are mostly obsolete, and the very definition of the term requires refinement and reinterpretation. A new arms control framework designed for a new world is urgently needed.[1]

In the years that followed the fall of the Berlin Wall, traditional arms control did not die; indeed, for a moment, it appeared to flourish. The United States and Russia agreed to slash their strategic nuclear arsenals through the Strategic Arms Reductions Treaty (START) and made rapid progress toward a follow-on, START II, while simultaneous unilateral declarations by presidents George H. W. Bush and Boris Yeltsin led to deeply reduced deployment of tactical nuclear weapons, particularly by the United States. South Africa destroyed its nuclear weapons and joined the Nuclear Non-Proliferation Treaty (NPT). Belarus, Ukraine, and Kazakhstan relinquished their shares of the former Soviet nuclear arsenal; Brazil and Argentina abandoned nuclear programs and joined the NPT as well. By 2004, only ten countries were believed to have nuclear weapons or well-advanced programs, in contrast with sixteen in the 1980s and twenty-one in the 1960s.[2] North Korea (the DPRK) and the United States negotiated the Agreed Framework, which constrained and aimed ultimately to end North Korea's nuclear capabilities. Russia acknowledged the existence of its clandestine biological weapons program and agreed to eliminate it, while the world's leading powers signed and ratified the Chemical Weapons Convention, banning chemical weapons worldwide. Nongovernmental organizations built support for a treaty banning land mines, and much of the world signed up.

These successes came on the heels of a host of cold war arms control accomplishments. The Limited Test Ban Treaty, Outer Space Treaty, and Antarctic Treaty had removed areas of possible military competition that could have been hard for either superpower to resist had the other not done so too. The Anti-Ballistic Missile (ABM) Treaty and a series of hotline agreements had helped reduce the danger of a crisis turning into a hot war, as their drafters intended, at a time when missile defense had little prospect of significantly reducing the damage from any potential nuclear conflict.[3] (Debate admittedly continues about whether Ronald Reagan's Strategic Defense Initiative—which would eventually have collided with the ABM Treaty—contributed to the fall of the Soviet regime.)[4] The Nuclear Non-Proliferation Treaty helped avoid runaway proliferation in the 1970s and 1980s.

During the cold war, taking part in arms control negotiations also allowed top U.S. and Soviet officials to develop personal ties at a time when tensions were high and finding alternative means of interacting was difficult. Both sides recognized that personal relationships could be useful for calming nerves and easing communication during crises. Some in the West put too much stock in these personal relationships and let down their guard against the potential Soviet threat, which did not disappear as a result of arms control and détente. And arms control had other important shortcomings—it did little to meaningfully limit the number of nuclear and conventional arms deployed by the superpowers or to dampen low-level conflict in the developing world. But its accomplishments were important too. And the contacts it fostered were beneficial and recognized as such by most policymakers from both major American political parties.[5]

Yet whatever its cold war legacy and whatever momentum it carried into the 1990s, arms control began to founder as the century wound down. In 1998, India and Pakistan tested nuclear weapons, despite the existence of the Nuclear Non-Proliferation Treaty (these two countries were among the last holdouts) and the Comprehensive Test Ban Treaty, which was still open to new signatories. In that same year, North Korea fired long-range missiles, highlighting the absence of any formal multilateral restrictions on long-range delivery vehicles, and Iraq toyed with United Nations weapons inspectors searching the country for chemical and biological weapons, leading the inspectors to terminate the UN mission. Although the United States and Russia signed the START II treaty, successive delays in ratification prevented it from ever going into effect. The U.S. Senate rejected the Comprehensive Test Ban Treaty in 1999, and at the decade's end, the days of the Anti-Ballistic Missile Treaty were numbered (see the appendix for synopses of these and other treaties).

Amid this decline, President George W. Bush entered office accompanied by advisers who were overwhelmingly opposed to most forms of traditional arms control. Such complete lack of nostalgia for cold war treaties helped them dismiss approaches that appeared to have outlived their usefulness. In the president's first year in office, he abandoned negotiations on START III and committed the United States to withdrawing from the ABM Treaty. In 2002, he signed the Moscow Treaty, requiring the United States and Russia to cut their deployed strategic nuclear arsenals to between 1,700 and 2,200 warheads by the end of 2012, but the treaty was notable for its lack of detail and of binding, monitored provisions. President Bush also chose to reject the Ottawa Convention banning land mines and the Comprehensive Test Ban Treaty, while shunning further negotiations on the monitoring protocol of the Biological Weapons Convention. As the president took these actions, his administration worked to develop a spirit of partnership with the government of President Vladimir Putin of Russia, especially after the September 11, 2001, terrorist attacks. In this way, Bush attempted to demonstrate that, at least in many aspects, U.S.-Russian relations had reached a point where arms control negotiations and treaties were no longer needed to facilitate diplomatic interaction or to ensure cooperation.[6]

In that, the president was right. But the Bush administration did not develop a new framework to replace the old one. It did show leadership on a few specific and important issues. Most creatively, it promoted a loose coalition known as the Proliferation Security Initiative, which aimed at interdicting shipments of materials used in developing weapons of mass destruction (WMD), particularly in the coastal waters of participating countries. And it proposed prohibiting access to nuclear power technologies that could also be used in nuclear weapons programs by any countries not already possessing those technologies.

However, given the small size of much dangerous weaponry and equipment and thus the difficulty of finding and tracking it, attempts at interdiction alone are insufficient to meet the massive and mounting threat of WMD proliferation. And the administration's approach to tightening access to nuclear-related technologies asks a great deal of less developed countries without offering much in return. While unobjectionable if it could be realized, the proposal seems unlikely to be acceptable to much of the world and thus unlikely to be particularly effective.

Most controversially, the Bush administration adopted the option of preventive war for thwarting the proliferation of weapons of mass destruction—often promoted as a doctrine of preemption. But preventive war, while occasionally appropriate, is a tool that can do as much to spur proliferation as to contain it. The administration's doctrine also appears to have weakened Washington's ability to build strong international coalitions to deal with security problems like proliferation.

The United States and the world thus still need a new strategy for controlling dangerous technologies in an age of terror. The tragic events of September 11 awoke Americans to the arrival of that age and put an emphatic end to the transition period between the end of the cold war and whatever strategic era was to come next. This does not appear to be, as some had predicted, an age dominated by U.S.-Chinese rivalry. Nor is it the "End of History," when large-scale violence and strong ideological struggle are mostly confined to the developing world. It will also not be the age of world government or global confederation. Some of these possibilities may have their day decades in the future, but not yet. The current period in American and broader Western foreign policy must first be one of controlling terrorists, rogues, and the technologies that can make them so dangerous.

Still, to develop broad international support, which is needed to maximize cooperation and reduce the number of problem cases, a new arms control framework must serve the interests of other countries as well as those of the United States. In particular, to the extent possible it should address civil conflict. Severely exacerbated by small arms and financed by illicit resource trading from Africa to Latin America to Central and Southeast Asia, such conflict continues to take hundreds of thousands of lives each year and creates a breeding ground for terrorists and their financiers. Arms control alone will not solve this problem; indeed, it is at best a secondary and supporting instrument of policy. But it can help. If the United States shows a commitment to use this and other policy tools—such as military training, humanitarian assistance, diplomacy, and, in extreme cases, multilateral armed intervention—to address the security needs of non-Western countries, it will attract broader support for America's overall arms control agenda. Given the role that failed and warring states play in global terrorism, it will also directly benefit U.S. security.

While they often contain valuable ideas, too many of the more prominent proposals for arms control would ignore these basic realities and thus lead the United States down the wrong path. Assessing them provides a useful way to begin constraining future arms control choices.

At one extreme, some argue explicitly that the procedures and substance of U.S.-Soviet cold war arms control should be resuscitated. Debate over the 2002 Moscow Treaty on strategic offensive arms reflected this desire, as many critics lamented what had become of superpower arms control. Though the critiques of the treaty differed, their common theoretical underpinning was concern that, in contrast with previous nuclear weapons accords, this treaty would provide little future predictability regarding stockpile size and composition. For example, the never-ratified and now defunct START II Treaty had contained detailed limitations on missiles with multiple warheads and strategic bombers, while the Moscow Treaty contained only an aggregate limit. Some argued that the new ambiguity would force both the United States and Russia to hedge, resulting in larger and more menacing arsenals.[7] Such arguments, however, rest on the assumption that each nation's decisions about sizing and structuring its nuclear arsenal are based directly on the size and structure of the other's arsenal. This type of sizing is increasingly less prevalent, as the end of the cold war permeates both countries' bureaucracies. Rather than assuming that the shape of one side's forces determines the shape of the other's and investing efforts in more detailed U.S.-Russian arms control, further efforts should be directed at shaking up the nuclear planning establishments, breaking them of their residual cold war habits.

If some would return to cold war arms control, others would abandon arms control altogether. Indeed, some arms control critics dismiss not only cold war paradigms, but also the entire enterprise of negotiating controls on dangerous weapons and technologies. This is a mistake. It ignores the seriousness of the global threats that arms control attempts to address while overestimating the universal applicability of other policy tools, such as military force or unilateral sanctions. Indeed, whatever their rhetoric, even most critics of arms control implicitly recognize that fact. For example, few openly dismiss the value of establishing supplier cartels for sensitive technologies, banning the possession of weapons of mass destruction by other states, or disarming radical regimes by targeted efforts that leverage international taboos against chemical and biological arms.

The alternatives to some sort of arms control—interdiction, blockades, and military action, carried out unilaterally or by coalitions of the willing—are not up to the task of controlling dangerous arms. Each of these activities may be necessary at some point, but alone—and even as a group—they will be insufficient. Limited attacks to disarm countries will often prove impossible because of insufficient intelligence about the location of key enemy assets.[8] All-out invasions to overthrow offending regimes are hugely difficult and risky; in some cases they would be even more so than in Iraq in 2003.[9]

More fundamentally, were the set of countries pursuing advanced weapons of mass destruction to significantly expand, even the United States and its close allies would not have the financial, human, or political capital necessary to forcibly restrain them. Coercive instruments of policy can work only in a rather small number of cases, given the diplomatic and military difficulty of employing them. Arms control cannot provide absolute guarantees that countries will not acquire or sell dangerous materials. But it can provide disincentives to such actions, make it more difficult to carry them out, and make it easier to detect illicit activity. By doing so, it can also help to establish predicates, if necessary, for coercive action. Indeed, arms control can and should be viewed as a complement to coercive action, not as a substitute for it.

Cooperative controls on dangerous technologies and weapons might not be needed were the world clearly and permanently separated into two classes, incorrigible bad actors and well-intentioned good states. In such a world, arms control might indeed have little relevance. When they could, good states would simply be compelled to forcibly deny bad actors access to nuclear and advanced biological weapons. This clarity of vision is useful for confronting the world's worst regimes.[10] The world, however, also has many far more complex cases. During the last twenty years, countries like Brazil, Argentina, Sweden, Egypt, Taiwan, and South Korea have all explored and rejected the option of building nuclear weapons. For many if not most, the benefit of remaining or becoming members in good standing of the international community through accession and adherence to the NPT was an important influence on their decision.

Universal standards have important effects. They do not directly dissuade extremist states from pursuing weapons of mass destruction, but they can help the United States and the international community confront them when they do and make it harder for them to succeed. For example, it is striking that, despite the discord over how to deal with Saddam Hussein in 2003, world leaders were united in considering his possession of weapons of mass destruction unacceptable—and in having similar views toward North Korea's and Iran's nuclear programs. Internationally accepted standards and values can also affect the internal debates of countries such as India, South Africa, and Ukraine, at least at the margin. In a close call, that marginal difference can be important in leading them not to pursue, or not to use, capabilities such as nuclear weapons.

Of course, arms control can go too far, if it constrains American power in a way that limits the ability of the United States to act alone when genuinely necessary. Some have advocated arms control as a way of promoting the general spread of global governance. By constraining the power of the state, including that of the United States, they hope to transform the nature of sovereignty, reduce military expenditures, reduce the likelihood of war, alleviate pressures for proliferation, and establish a more cooperative international climate in which many global problems can be handled internationally.[11] Others advocate using arms control as a mechanism to improve American overseas relationships—especially in light of the harm that the war in Iraq has done to those relationships—without thinking clearly about whether a proposed treaty makes sense on security grounds.[12] But when arms control becomes strategically unrealistic or focused more on diplomatic process than on technical substance, it can be downright dangerous. In a worst case, it can fail just as spectacularly as it did after World War I, when impractical accords could not stop the rise of Nazi Germany (and may even have helped blind the international community to the stark challenge it presented). Less terribly but still dangerously, arms control could lead to unrealistically heightened expectations followed by great disappointment—just as when U.S.-Soviet détente, whatever its benefits, could not stop the Soviet military buildup and assertiveness of the 1970s or the temporary deterioration in superpower relations that followed.

To be sure, the nature of state sovereignty is changing in important ways. States already interact today in ways that are much different from those of the past, and their interaction will change in the future.[13] For example, issues of human rights, the environment, and public health within states are of much greater concern in a world characterized by large populations, extremely powerful technologies, shrinking resource bases, economic globalization, and rapid, easy travel and communications.[14]

But disarming or straitjacketing sovereign states too much can harm global stability, which still depends on a strong United States (and other powers) to prevent war; it can also harm American strategic interests.[15] Weakening or constraining the military forces of liberal democracies in inappropriate ways—such as by attempting to abolish nuclear weapons or by placing broad caps on great power deployments of conventional weapons—can reduce the kind of great power stability that the world generally benefits from today.[16] Perhaps civilization has advanced beyond the point where major countries would compete for influence and control if there were no clearly predominant power, as they did before the world wars and at many other times in history. But it hardly seems worth the risk of finding out by severely weakening the United States. Many countries criticize the United States, often with cause. But they also tend to want to ally with it; in the end, most have faith in its system of government and its broad role in the world. These realities have led to an unprecedented "bandwagoning" of the modern democracies onto a U.S.-led system of alliances involving close military and political collaboration.[17] This system has contributed enormously to peace among the great powers. In that way, it has accomplished a goal of arms control that Thomas Schelling has recently reemphasized—not simply eliminating arms or preventing their acquisition, but also preventing their use.[18]

Foundations for Arms Control

An enduring and effective arms control strategy must steer clear of these pitfalls while zeroing in on America's greatest security challenge: defending itself and others against catastrophic terrorism. Arms control can do that best by focusing on the world's most dangerous technologies, nuclear and biological arms, to prevent their spread to its most dangerous actors, extremist states and terrorist organizations. To do that, arms control must focus on three critical needs. It needs to provide early warning of when and where outlaw regimes might acquire dangerous weapons. It must integrate coercive enforcement action more intimately into its structure, to respond to situations in which extremist regimes or terrorist groups are detected pursuing illicit weaponry—and to deter them from doing so in the first place, where possible. And it must be harmonized with broader American foreign policy to help most states, particularly nonaggressive and democratic ones, feel greater confidence in their own security. This will reduce their inclination to seek dangerous arms and increase their willingness to stop countries that are so inclined. This last need will be successfully addressed not by nuclear disarmament, as envisioned in the NPT, but rather by means such as providing NATO-like security guarantees to states that might otherwise slide to the nuclear or biological brink. We elaborate on each of these ideas below.

Arms Control Needs Priorities

Modern arms control should, as its central organizing principle, attempt to prevent the spread of nuclear materials and biological pathogens. Most other purposes are secondary at best.

Any significant and worthwhile arms control effort will require a sustained high level of attention from at least the secretaries of state and defense and perhaps the president, not to mention much of the Congress. It is therefore important not to overload the agenda. Even if many accords on secondary issues could be marginally useful, it would often require a great deal of intellectual and political effort to assess and promote them. Given the host of other issues that policymakers must confront, expecting them to focus on scores of new arms control initiatives would be unwise. Indeed, it could be counterproductive, making arms control an excessive and unwelcome intrusion into the work of busy policymakers and fostering an image of arms control as a means of constraining legitimate and necessary state power.

The need to have a clear set of technological priorities should drive arms control analysts to focus primarily on the problem of nuclear and biological weapons. Of any class of arms, existing or foreseen, nuclear and biological weapons pose the greatest direct threats to American security. A single first-generation nuclear weapon with a yield of twenty kilotons, detonated at ground level in Manhattan at midday, could kill upward of 500,000 people.[19] Larger thermonuclear weapons could kill millions. An attack with biological agents might kill even more than a single first-generation weapon—for example, if effective civil defense is lacking, an attack on Washington, D.C., with 100 kilograms of high-grade anthrax spores could cause more than a million deaths.[20] And because of the revolution in biotechnology, the technology needed to engineer pathogens to be more virulent, more robust, and more lethal is becoming widely available.

In contrast, a well-executed attack with 1,000 kilograms of sarin gas, a relatively effective chemical weapon, would kill several thousand at most.[21] A radiological weapon would be unlikely to kill many more than those hit by the conventional blast used to disperse radioactive materials, even including deaths from cancer, and would kill hundreds at most.[22] Different delivery vehicles—cruise and ballistic missiles or advanced combat aircraft—are certainly threatening, but without being mated to powerful weapons of mass destruction they generally offer enemies little ability to directly threaten Americans. Space and information weapons might provide military leverage in the future, but unless coupled to lethal technologies like nuclear weapons they have little prospect of causing mass carnage (assuming certain homeland security efforts are made).

To prevent terrorists and extremist states from gaining dangerous technologies, an arms control agenda must continue to stanch the spread of extremely dangerous technologies and arms to all states. Following India's nuclear test in 1974, strategic analysts worried about a world in which scores of countries would possess nuclear weapons—what Albert Wohlstetter termed the "nuclear-armed crowd."[23] Similar worries abound today not only of a world widely armed with nuclear weapons, but also of one in which sophisticated biological weapons are widely proliferated. Such a world would be far more prone to catastrophe than the world we live in now, no matter which states possessed such arms. Some have argued that the carefully managed spread of massively destructive weapons would be stabilizing.[24] This argument is unpersuasive. Any state that acquires nuclear weapons must confront the prospect of nuclear errors—including the theft of nuclear weapons by terrorists—which are far more likely in a state with a nascent nuclear arsenal than an established one.[25] Moreover, while possession of a nuclear arsenal might provide a state some measure of protection against external attack, its vulnerability while it sought nuclear weapons could invite the external attack its desired arsenal was designed to deter, especially in a crisis. A similar analysis applies to biological arms.

Indeed, proliferation must be stopped or rolled back whenever possible, including even in friendly states. And the growing talk in some quarters that countries such as Germany or Japan should consider their nuclear options in the future should be challenged forcefully. As Joseph Nye noted more than two decades ago, "The great danger is the exponential curve of 'speculative fever'—an accelerating change in rate. In such a situation, general restraints break down and decisions to forbear are reconsidered because 'everyone is doing it.'"[26] The fact that past proliferation has not set off such a chain reaction provides little comfort; merely because the world has been lucky does not mean it should again take the risk of setting off a future speculative fever. In recent years, the only states openly suspected of advanced attempts to acquire nuclear weapons—Iran, Iraq, and North Korea—were widely viewed as backward countries. But if a country like Germany or Japan were to acquire nuclear weapons, the example would change. (Indeed, the nuclear tests of India and Pakistan in 1998 have already exacerbated the danger.) Germany and Japan provide "examples of countries achieving significant status in world politics without nuclear weaponry."[27] Were such countries to pursue nuclear weapons, many weak, unstable states might decide that to be players on the world stage, they too must acquire nuclear weapons.

Arms Control Should Produce Transparency and Early Warning

Like so much else in a rapidly globalizing world, dangerous technology can spread more quickly and more quietly than before. Instead of requiring a new Manhattan Project to develop nuclear arms, a state might now buy much of the necessary technology from rogue states or freelance vendors, as underscored by the sales over more than a decade of Pakistani nuclear secrets to Libya, North Korea, and Iran. Instead of requiring a massive, deliberate mobilization of scientific and engineering resources, production of biological organisms of increased virulence and lethality can be done covertly—or even inadvertently. This acceleration of weapons acquisition leaves the world with little time to react and fewer options once a proliferation-related development is detected—and with an associated reduction in the chance of reversing the advance.

One goal of arms control, then, should be to enable early detection of dangerous developments. Whether cooperative or coercive tools are used for achieving compliance with restrictions, early warning—and hence possible early action—will make them more likely to be effective.

Outside the realm of cooperative arms control, technical means for detecting proliferation activities need to be improved. But the potential of technology will be limited, given the small physical signatures of properly contained biological operations as well as of shielded nuclear materials. As a result, demands on countries for active transparency—through inspections and intrusive monitoring, for example—will need to be increased. As the technical capacity of states to hide proliferation activities (especially in the biological realm) outpaces the capabilities of outside states to detect them, the burden of opening up and demonstrating the absence of illegal activities must shift to the state of concern.

Arms control will also have to face the problem of intent—even when a state is known to have certain dangerous equipment, it may be impossible to tell whether that equipment is for peaceful or illicit use until it is too late. To confront this danger, arms control will have to constrain more tightly the proliferation of dual-use technologies, no matter what their stated application—not normally banning them but often strongly regulating or limiting their use and availability.

Arms Control Should Be a Complement to Military Force

In its cold war conceptualization, arms control was necessarily viewed as a means of avoiding war among great powers. It was one element of a strategy designed explicitly as an alternative to war. Yet in the new era of advanced technology and terrorism, war among great powers is no longer the greatest security threat to the United States or many other countries. Moreover, there may now be situations in which, paradoxically, war in the near term is preferable to an illusory peace—and in which arms control can help establish the legal, moral, and strategic predicates for taking coercive steps, including military action. This is particularly true for war against relatively small, extremist states violating their international obligations not to engage in proliferation of dangerous technology. The costs of war to both the United States and the world are often less than they would have been in any U.S.-Soviet war, and the risks of allowing dangerous regimes to remain in power may be greater. In other words, the use of military force to destroy illicit weapons or overthrow a regime may be both more practical and more desirable than it would have been during the cold war.

This is not by any stretch meant as a blanket endorsement for preemptive or preventive military strikes by the international community. Nor should military force be the first coercive instrument to which nations turn when confronting a dangerous state. It should generally be a last resort—or at least a resort turned to only when other possible measures are unpromising or when waiting would be too dangerous.

But with these caveats noted, the central point—that enforcement must be integral to arms control—remains valid. States that refuse to provide the transparency described earlier and to refrain from unacceptably dangerous or ambiguous behavior must be held to account. That is true whether their offending behavior extends over a long period or whether they suddenly seek to abandon previous nonproliferation commitments, for example, by withdrawing from the NPT. Nor should participation in key accords be seen as optional; it is critical that the United States and other countries promote and reaffirm the generally prevailing belief that nonproliferation of weapons of mass destruction is an obligation on all states, not a choice. The details of how to respond to any violators should be determined by the likely costs and benefits of the situation at hand. But all options, up to and including regime change, should be on the table in extreme cases.[28] Arms control should thus serve both to establish high standards of transparency and behavior and to allow ample time for the international community to confront a noncompliant regime before it can obtain or use the most dangerous weaponry. By agreeing on those standards in advance, the international community is far more likely to be able to agree on when coercive enforcement has become necessary. If it can convey its resolve to potential proliferators, arms control can have the even more desirable effect of deterring proliferation in the first place.

Arms Control Must Address the Security of Nations That Do Not Have Weapons of Mass Destruction

For several decades, the world's nuclear powers have understood that they must offer other states incentives not to pursue nuclear arms of their own. The 1968 Nuclear Non-Proliferation Treaty encoded such a bargain; the nuclear powers offered other states access to nuclear energy technology and also committed themselves to their own eventual nuclear disarmament.

Whatever their merits during the cold war, however, neither incentive is sufficient today. The nuclear powers need not rescind their pledge of eventual nuclear disarmament; perhaps in the very distant future complete disarmament might be desirable and feasible. But fulfilling that pledge is not a realistic objective for the coming decades. If the world's great powers were to abolish their nuclear weapons, it could weaken deterrence and invite unwanted instability while not even addressing most of the security pressures that might make states seek nuclear weapons. And economic incentives can never substitute for robust national security incentives. Few governments in the world can put any other issue ahead of protecting the physical well-being of the state; certainly no American government ever could. If the United States seeks to deny countries certain arms and technologies in the interest of bolstering its security, it needs a serious strategy to help other countries ensure their own. Otherwise, too many states will seek dangerous arms for their own protection, and the enforcement scheme described above will be overwhelmed.

To prevent this, arms control must be explicitly linked to broader American security policy. The United States and its allies should offer to create new security guarantees and in some cases perhaps even new alliance systems, tailored to specific circumstances, for democratic, peaceful countries in other parts of the world. Under some circumstances it can and should offer security guarantees to states that fall somewhat short of that description. These would have to be broad and public assurances, promising U.S. and other allied assistance in repelling any unprovoked external assaults against a country's territorial integrity.

Security assurances like those offered by Russia, the United States, and the United Kingdom to Ukraine when it gave up its nuclear weapons may sometimes be adequate. Those countries promised not to attack Ukraine and further pledged to seek immediate U.N. Security Council action to provide assistance to Ukraine if it ever were attacked.[29]

A more recent example is the Bush administration's stated willingness to offer North Korea a form of security assurance in exchange for denuclearization. Offering this type of accord to a pariah state with a recent history of egregiously oppressing its own people is a more delicate matter, in that it would deprive the United States of the option of using force for humanitarian or other purposes and could place arms control ahead of all other American foreign policy objectives. Such an approach, poorly constructed, may even undermine broader arms control goals, potentially encouraging other states to develop nuclear programs in order to extract security pledges from the outside world. However, in situations where no good preemptive or coercive options exist, such an accord may make the best of a bad situation—as long as it is carefully conditioned on the behavior of the country in question.

In other cases, security assurances that go much further and provide a more binding NATO-like pledge by the United States and others to treat an attack on a given country as an attack on themselves may be appropriate and required. If the United States is to continue to argue that it needs nuclear weapons and massive military power for its own security, it must offer a vision of equal security to any other nation that respects human rights and avoids violence.

This concept is broad—but it is not radical. Although inconsistently applied in the past, it has been at the core of U.S. security policy since World War II. From that time onward, the United States has formed alliances or close security partnerships (of admittedly varying strength and success) in Europe, Latin America, East Asia, the Pacific, and the Middle East. Today, it has close security partnerships with some seventy countries. The difference is that during the cold war, such alliances were designed to provide extended deterrence (using conventional and if necessary nuclear means) against a global communist threat. Today they are important for a set of more diffuse security challenges, varying from region to region and country to country. But a key thread running through them all is the American sense of realism that acknowledges other countries' legitimate security interests and attempts to address them using security guarantees.

This policy need not be adopted everywhere at once or in the same way. NATO's criteria for admitting a new member require the applicant country to be a democracy and to have a civilian-controlled military and a nonaggressive foreign policy; the country also must commit itself to contributing to the common defense. That a country comply with these NATO requirements should be a goal, though not a strict condition, of any new security arrangements. Several of the countries that may need security assurances in the coming years, such as a number of Persian Gulf monarchies, are not democracies. Ideally, in such cases security assurances would be given on the condition that countries at least make progress toward participatory governance. Also, as a practical matter the United States would have to handle certain cases very carefully, such as countries bordering Russia (where, if recent history is a guide, Russia might resist). It should also partner with other strong states in offering these relationships to reduce the American burden and to minimize political vulnerability.

But as a vision for future security relations, this collective security concept holds out a cogent and intellectually consistent alternative to the unrealistic goals of abolishing nuclear weapons or making unequal security arrangements. It allows the United States to do what it must, which is to maintain a substantial stockpile of nuclear weapons and its overwhelming military strength, without hypocritically, and thus ultimately unsustainably, demanding that other countries accept a lower standard of national security.

Arms Control Criteria for Today's World

Four decades ago, Thomas Schelling and Morton Halperin set forth the principles that would dominate the arms control consensus for the duration of the cold war. In their seminal book, *Strategy and Arms Control*, they defined arms control as "all the forms of military cooperation between potential enemies in the interest of reducing the likelihood of war, its scope and violence if it occurs, and the political and economic costs of being prepared for it."[30] With these three goals as guides, they set out to find the concrete forms arms control should take in their bipolar world. Their resulting analysis focused on ways to prevent accidental nuclear war and to slow or stop the then accelerating arms race.

Today, the United States faces a decidedly different world. The United States is the world's predominant military power, with any potential peer competitor at least decades away from challenging it. Almost all of America's greatest immediate threats come not from the strength of another state, as they did during the cold war, but from relatively weak states and terrorist organizations. Arms control needs to accept these new realities and work within them to enhance American security. That does not mean Schelling and Halperin are now wrong, only that the geostrategic foundation on which they—and American policymakers—built their construct for arms control is gone. It makes sense to emulate their approach, which explicitly subordinated arms control strategy to broader security strategy. But that approach needs to be adapted to today's circumstances, not used as an excuse for clinging to decades-old conclusions or, conversely, for rejecting arms control altogether.

It should be clear already that the goals of arms control must change—and that so must the conception of acceptable methods of control. Halperin and Schelling's restrictive requirement that arms control must involve "military cooperation between potential enemies" made sense during the cold war. Such a formulation was automatic for a program conceived during the height of the superpower conflict, when aggressive confrontation with the enemy, Russia, was unthinkable. In contrast, today military confrontation in the pursuit of arms control is indeed thinkable and in some cases possible—the 2003 war in Iraq is but one example. The United States now pursues arms control with Russia, not because it suspects that the Russians have ill intent toward the United States, but to keep Russia's weapons out of the hands of terrorists. Arms control, then, must encompass not only cooperative arrangements among adversaries, but also cooperative arrangements among friends. Most of all, it must be an integral part of a strategy toward especially dangerous enemies that establishes transparent criteria for coercive action, and hence the predicate for action, when those enemies violate international principles or engage in other dangerous behavior.[31] Often, this approach will deter proliferation before it occurs.

Certain situations may still call for cold war–style arms control. For example, as we discuss later, confidence-building measures might be pursued between India and Pakistan and conventional arms control might work on the Korean Peninsula. Nonetheless, U.S. arms control strategy needs new foundations and new guidance. In summary, we propose three new goals to guide future arms control efforts:

—Prevent the spread of the world's most dangerous technologies, focusing on terrorists and states that might aid them.

—Create political predicates for coercive action to contain, manage, or reverse proliferation should it occur.

—Improve security from war and terrorism for peoples and states not actively hostile to the United States.

The first goal leads naturally to a focus on nuclear and biological technologies, because they are the world's most dangerous. It also means that preventing proliferation of weapons to terrorists or weak states will normally take precedence over constraining great power arsenals, in the rare instances that those two goals are in conflict. The second goal directs the United States to integrate coercive action and arms control in new ways.

It also leads to an emphasis on transparency, which will be needed to determine which states should be targeted for coercive action. The third goal points out that arms control will not succeed unless all peaceful countries possess a viable vision for enhancing their security.

The days of cold war arms control are gone for good. The future of arms control must be based on the clear understanding that today's strategic environment is characterized more by the problem of weak states and dangerous nonstate actors than by competition among the great powers. Arms control should harness American military power as a force for good that should not, as an end, be constrained by treaty, although it should be wielded very carefully. In the past, fully formed arsenals were the primary danger; today, dangerous enabling technologies are the greatest worry. These are new and fundamental changes. They mean that the organizing principles of the business of arms control, and the priorities of policymakers, need a fresh focus for the age of terror.

CHAPTER 2

Traditional Strategic Arms Control

Because they have been at the center of arms control thinking for so long, traditional strategic issues—including great power nuclear arsenals, missile defenses, and space systems—are a natural place to begin. That said, while they are hardly irrelevant, they generally are not top priorities for future arms control, with the important exception of ensuring that nuclear materials and warheads are not vulnerable to theft or transfer.

Many supporters of traditional arms control have expressed dismay at what has happened to the process of negotiating and implementing strategic arms accords, particularly between the U.S. and Russia. The strongest complaints have concerned the abandonment of the START process, which addressed U.S. and Russian strategic arms; the lack of binding mechanisms in the 2002 Moscow Treaty between the United States and Russia on offensive arms reductions; the demise of the ABM Treaty in the same year; and the potential for an arms race in outer space. Proponents of deeper bilateral arms control typically cite three reasons for reversing these shifts. First, some refer to classic stability calculations to argue that, for example, an antiballistic missile (ABM) ban stabilizes the bilateral relationship or that restrictions on MIRVed missiles (a START II provision) mitigate policymakers' worries about a possible first strike. Second, others argue that arms reductions must be made transparent and verifiable if they are to serve as the basis for deeper reductions by both the United States and Russia; without such certainty, they argue, planners will have to work with worst-case assumptions, eviscerating any effectiveness of the treaties being pursued. Third, some suggest that advances made in the U.S.-Russian relationship through further arms control will allow the United States to more easily make progress in other relationships—for example, its trilateral relationship with Russia and China.

The stability calculations made during the cold war no longer mean much, however, because the underlying political relationship between the United States and Russia has fundamentally changed. Initiatives like the Nunn-Lugar Cooperative Threat Reduction program can, if structured properly, provide adequate transparency and verifiability without formal treaties.[1] And many other means now exist to tighten U.S.-Russian relations.

One argument in favor of traditional U.S.-Russian arms control does have some merit—that continued U.S. and Russian reductions can help diminish the importance of nuclear weapons as an instrument of security policy in the modern world and thus influence other nations' proliferation decisions, as well as the nuclear buildup decisions of countries such as the People's Republic of China (PRC). Indeed, it is difficult for Washington to successfully preach to the rest of the world that nuclear weapons are unnecessary when it—along with others—keeps large arsenals and even develops doctrine envisioning new uses for nuclear weapons. Demonstrating that the United States sees nuclear weapons as less and less useful is thus important.

That said, there are significant limits to how much force of example matters. First, the ultimate goal of article VI of the Nuclear Non-Proliferation Treaty, complete disarmament, is entirely unrealistic for the foreseeable future, given the security risks inherent in American denuclearization, the greater risk of conventional conflict that a denuclearized world might conceivably face, and the technical barriers to verifying that a nation has abolished it nuclear weapons. Given this initial constraint, the ability of the nuclear superpowers to promote restraint among other countries through force of example alone will be limited. Second, and even more important, most states make their decisions about acquiring nuclear weapons primarily on the basis of their immediate security environment, together with calculations of the diplomatic and economic costs of doing so. Disarmament can influence the latter somewhat, through force of example and creation of norms, but only at the margin.

Contemporary arms control should focus on the world's most dangerous technologies and weapons, not the most symbolically important or historically familiar. As a rule, therefore, since today traditional U.S.-Russian nuclear arms control offers at best only modest benefits, it should receive less emphasis than in the past. A second Moscow treaty cutting long-range offensive forces further would be worthwhile for the symbolic benefits of having Russia and the United States continue to deemphasize the role of nuclear weapons in modern international security. But these benefits do not warrant making negotiation of any accord the centerpiece of U.S.-Russian relations, which in the nuclear security realm should focus on matters of more central concern to both sides, such as cooperative threat reduction and export controls. Nonproliferation efforts could still succeed if such an accord is not attempted or cannot be concluded. As with the 2002 Moscow Treaty, a second, if concluded, should be kept short and simple. More important in the U.S.-Russian nuclear relationship are the efforts discussed in the next chapter, such as improved export controls and the Nunn-Lugar program, which is designed to improve the physical security of weapons-usable material and nuclear warheads.

The Comprehensive Test Ban Treaty (CTBT) is worthwhile and ought to be ratified by the U.S. Senate. If American politicians and government officials cannot resolve the U.S. position on CTBT, however, the United States can greatly mitigate the downsides of not ratifying the treaty by continuing its moratorium on testing and making a decision not to develop new types of warheads. As argued below, new warheads promise no significant military benefits.

But such legacy issues with enduring importance are few. There is no pressing reason for a new missile defense accord to replace the ABM Treaty. Whatever strategic damage may have resulted from the Bush administration's decision to withdraw from the ABM Treaty has been limited, and designing a new accord that constrains defenses would be complicated, if possible at all. That said, there is a case for a different sort of arms control—informal U.S. unilateral restraint in Washington's future decisions to deploy missile defenses. Keeping deployments limited in scope and out of outer space would reduce the chances of a setback in U.S.-Russian or U.S.-Chinese relations; moreover, a limited defense is all that technology can hope to achieve in the near future against extremist countries with small arsenals.

As for other possible controls on space weaponry, some specific restrictions would make sense, but in general restricting weapons in space should not be the next great frontier of arms control. To be sure, the United States would not benefit from any hasty move to put weapons in orbit or to develop ground-based systems focused specifically on targeting objects in space; thus it should eschew advanced development, testing, production, and deployment of systems dedicated to such purposes. But it is also not realistic or desirable to seek formalized bans on most types of space weapons, except on the testing and use of debris-producing weapons. For one thing, verification of compliance with a ban is very difficult, especially when dealing with possible antisatellite (ASAT) weaponry such as microsatellites. Second, even some ground-based American missile defense programs have inherent ASAT potential and the same could soon be true of other countries' programs, making ASAT bans inherently ambiguous and impractical. Third, the United States might someday need the ability to target enemy satellites—for example, if they were being used to target American aircraft carriers in time of war and could not be neutralized in a benign, reversible fashion.

Strategic Nuclear Arms Control

Formal arms accords have less to offer as a means of controlling strategic nuclear weaponry than in the past. It would be a mistake to attempt to return to previous approaches. Deeply detailed, traditional treaties are no longer needed to spur further cuts in U.S. and Russian nuclear arsenals. That said, informal accords between Moscow and Washington confirming limits on offensive arms can reinforce the generally positive paths that the nuclear superpowers are on already. China's arsenal is also an important concern, but arms control accords offer little prospect for productively controlling it and should not be attempted at this time. The United States would be well served to ratify the Comprehensive Test Ban Treaty and eschew development of fundamentally new types of nuclear weapons, but even if it does not ratify the CTBT, it can gain many of the same benefits by maintaining its existing moratorium on testing. The United States would also benefit from a unilateral systematic de-alerting of its nuclear forces, were such an action to spur reciprocating measures from Russia, but a treaty is probably not needed for this purpose.

Strategic Nuclear Arms

Today the state of nuclear relations among the great powers is sound. France and Britain remain content with maintaining modest deterrents to attack. China is enhancing its forces, but at a conservative pace consistent with the growth of the country's overall economy and defense budget and with a focus on modernization instead of expansion. The United States and Russia no longer view each other as true nuclear competitors. To be sure, elements in the strategic community on each side remain worried about the other, and thirty years of debate over missile defenses has in some cases cemented an outdated logic that has subsequently proven hard to revise. There are legitimate worries that a future Russian government could revert to having great concern about the details of the strategic balance—potentially a major problem, especially as the United States actually deploys strategic defenses in the years ahead. Russia's new first-use doctrine also is troubling and should not be condoned by U.S. policymakers.

On balance, though, nuclear dynamics are not upsetting the political relations among great powers today. The demise of the ABM Treaty has not caused the fallout many expected.[2] There are still concerns that Russia or China could find the actual deployment of proven defense systems by the United States more upsetting than its diplomatic decision to withdraw from a specific treaty. But the likely difficulties of developing missile defenses and the costs of doing so suggest that large-scale deployments will be far off. Still, even today's embryonic U.S. deployment plans could drive up the number of Chinese strategic missiles at least modestly relative to what they would have otherwise been.[3] This would affect the United States primarily through any domino effect it might cause in Asia, but it is not worrisome enough to justify a new treaty.

The 2002 Moscow Treaty, limiting Russia and the United States to 1,700 to 2,200 operational strategic warheads (for a brief moment in 2012), appears to be a reassuring guidepost for both countries in planning their nuclear forces and a stabilizing factor in their relationship. That is true even though its teeth are largely missing—beyond the aggregate numbers in 2012, few details are provided—and some arms control advocates found it wanting for that reason.[4] Although its stipulations technically apply for only a brief moment before the treaty expires (since there is no mandated schedule for incremental reductions between the treaty's ratification and that time), building forces back up to previous levels—which would require removing missiles from cold storage, as well as, most likely, building large numbers of new missiles—would take time. It would also take money that neither side seems likely to choose to spend on restoring its nuclear arsenal. Moreover, the two sides should not bemoan the loss of specific force structure constraints, as were contained in each START agreement—though force structure still matters for each country independently, it has little effect on their bilateral relationship, whose stability for the foreseeable future will be determined far more by broader matters than the nuclear balance.

Meanwhile, both the United States and Russia are dramatically reducing their emphasis on strategic nuclear forces, particularly within the context of their bilateral relationship—budgetarily, doctrinally, and politically. The strategic nuclear relationship has faded from salience in the post–cold war world, and that is all to the good, given that the two countries are not adversaries and that the nuclear balance between them should not matter. Even though Russia's 2000 national security doctrine, which prominently and emphatically reserves the right to use nuclear weapons first during a conflict, heightened the potential role of nuclear weapons in ensuring state security, and even though the United States therefore should disapprove of it, the doctrine appears motivated by a desire to repel armed aggression by regional competitors rather than to counter American forces. It was not designed to jockey, as during the cold war, for global influence through nuclear strength.[5]

The United States would benefit from a Moscow II arrangement that would push for lower numbers, whether in a permanent, binding way or not, whether limiting warhead inventories or just delivery vehicles. Ideally it would cut U.S. and Russian forces to 1,000 to 1,500 warheads each, including tactical nuclear warheads, and require dismantling most or all excess warhead stocks.[6]

There is little not to like about such a possible Moscow II agreement, whether formal or informal, ratified or not, rigorously verified or not. It could recommit the two states toward slightly lowering their number of weapons and their nuclear expenditures. If it reassured certain constituencies in each country, it could also sustain or even enhance cooperation on other matters, such as the Nunn-Lugar cooperative threat reduction efforts and coordination of export controls. It could also reassure the U.S. Congress and the Russian Duma, reducing the likelihood that they would pass legislation such as that passed by the United States in the mid-1990s that precluded cutting American forces until Russia agreed to make similar cuts.

That said, there is little be gained by pushing bilateral arms control much further, and a number of strategic complications could result from doing so. Arms reductions beyond those stipulated by the Moscow Treaty would have minimal impact on the broader nonproliferation regime. Although the Nuclear Non-Proliferation Treaty commits the United

States to long-term nuclear force reductions, ending reductions will not by itself drive states to go nuclear. As we argue in chapter 3, however, the most powerful incentive for participating in the nonproliferation regime will almost certainly be the perceived direct security benefits of doing so; unless states see superpower strategic weapons as a major security threat, U.S. and Russian arms cuts will not be a major asset in advancing nonproliferation. To be sure, moves to emphasize and increase the role of nuclear weapons could drive proliferation, since they encourage states to conclude that nuclear weapons are useful. Failing to bring total numbers close to zero, however, will not have similar ramifications, as long as the gradual downward trend in the number and role of U.S. and Russian nuclear weapons continues.

Another round of informal cuts makes sense. Even nuclear superpower arsenals of 1,000 warheads each, counting deployed and nondeployed weapons as well as tactical warheads, would preserve many hypothetical response options besides city-busting.[7] But going much lower than 1,000 weapons each in the U.S. and Russian arsenals holds little appeal for the foreseeable future. It would raise difficult dilemmas about how to address China's future arsenal and whether to include the PRC in a future accord—and raising those questions prematurely could be harmful. Giving China a full seat at the negotiating table could award it strategic influence—and strategic confidence regarding Taiwan or other issues—that it might not attain on its own. Ignoring its potential nuclear growth could have similar consequences: if Moscow and Washington cut their forces to a level that the PRC felt it could approach, an arms race dynamic that is presently absent might result.[8]

Some would argue against these two claims, suggesting that awarding China a full seat at the table would give it a greater stake in supporting the international security system. But there are more pressing international arms control initiatives than those concerning traditional strategic issues on which China could productively take a prominent role. Indeed, not having been involved in previous nuclear arms limitation accords, China may not expect to be invited into negotiations with the United States and Russia anytime soon. Its greater concern may well be missile defense. In some ways, Russia's willingness to tolerate, without strong protests, the Bush administration's withdrawal from the ABM Treaty left China in the lurch. It probably expected Moscow to take the lead in making the Bush administration pay a diplomatic price for eliminating constraints on missile defense, perhaps helping to convince the United States to accept at least some constraints on future deployments. When President Putin did not do so and Europe said little either, China was left largely on its own to mount any international resistance to the decision. Chinese leaders appear to have determined that such a course of action would have been unproductive after September 11, 2001, and after the spring 2001 P-3 episode, in which a Chinese pilot forced down a nearby American reconnaissance aircraft and China held its crew for nearly two weeks. They also most likely realized that a hostile stance would work against their interests in fostering a reasonably stable and constructive relationship between China and the United States.

Still, China has more reasons to worry about its strategic balance with the United States than does Russia. It is China, not Russia, that could plausibly wind up in a war against the United States, given the nature of the dispute between Beijing and Washington over Taiwan. China probably does not believe that it needs nuclear parity to satisfy its security requirements in such a crisis, or it would presumably have already worked harder to expand its arsenal. But its leaders may feel that China benefits from having some capacity to mount a nuclear strike against the United States, at least in response to a U.S. first strike. They may also want Washington to worry that if China were losing a conventional war over Taiwan it would escalate the conflict to the nuclear level.

For these reasons, the size and character of any U.S. missile defense deployment do matter and are likely to prove to be contentious in the American debate. Some will argue that Washington does not owe Beijing the right to be able to easily retaliate against U.S. or Taiwanese targets, especially given that China has no moral right to go to war against a small nearby democracy (assuming again, as we do, that the most plausible path to war between the United States and the PRC is a crisis involving Taiwan). Others will favor a limited American missile defense deployment—in theory capable enough to deal with a rogue threat yet not capable enough to threaten Russia's or even China's nuclear weapons—and might be willing to codify such constraints in a formal or informal pact. But as a matter of technical reality, there is no prospect of missile defense deployments being able to defeat China's nuclear forces. China can surely develop the types of countermeasures needed to defeat any midcourse defense.[9] It can base its missile force deeply inland in a manner that would defeat boost-phase defenses not based in space (and space-based boost-phase defenses would be extremely expensive and vulnerable even if technically feasible). It can also very modestly expand its arsenal if necessary. As long as the American system is sized and scaled to respond to a North Korean or Iranian (rather than Chinese) offensive threat, there should be little danger of provoking an unwanted reaction. Certainly, no new ABM Treaty–like instrument should be necessary to codify this simple strategic balance.

The Nuclear Firebreak and New Nuclear Weapons

Not all nuclear weapons issues relate to the number of deployed weapons or to the U.S.-Russian relationship. The most important American actions with respect to the U.S. nuclear arsenal are to abstain from using nuclear weapons, and, secondarily, to downplay the role of nuclear weapons in U.S. doctrine—for example, by exercising restraint in developing or testing new nuclear weapons. American conventional military dominance would be undermined in a world where the use of nuclear weapons was accepted, leading to erosion of U.S. security. The use of nuclear weapons—or even their indiscriminately threatened use—would strengthen domestic actors in potential proliferator states that claim that nuclear weapons have military value and strategic weight. A weakened taboo against nuclear weapons would undermine support for enforcing nonproliferation obligations as well if, as we argued earlier, such taboos and norms are less important than other countries' immediate security concerns.

No new nuclear weapons concept shows military or deterrent promise significant enough to outweigh these arms control concerns. Four primary types of new nuclear weapons have been proposed: low-yield weapons, earth-penetrating weapons, enhanced radiation weapons, and agent-defeat weapons.[10]

Low-Yield Weapons

The first type, low-yield weapons, refers to bombs that would explode in the air with a power perhaps a hundred times smaller than that of the bomb used on Hiroshima. Some deterrence theorists argue that these bombs could fill a critical gap in explosive power between the least powerful nuclear weapons in the current arsenal and the most powerful conventional bombs.[11] They argue that if these are not developed, enemies might conclude that American leaders would be unwilling to launch any nuclear counterattack because they would be unwilling to inflict the large number of casualties that an existing nuclear weapon would cause. At the same time, they argue that America's conventional arsenal alone is not enough to deter potential enemies. Thus, they argue, low-yield nuclear weapons could fill a vacuum: they would scare enemies more than non-nuclear arms, while presenting a more credible threat to the enemy. This argument, however, is unconvincing, since the United States already has nuclear weapons as small as 300 tons and conventional bombs as large as 10 tons. A bomb of intermediate size—100 tons, for example—would confer few benefits. It would destroy an area only 30 percent smaller than a 300-ton bomb, thus not significantly increasing the credibility of the threat that it poses; at the same time, its blast effects could be approximately replicated by five 10-ton conventional bombs. Thus it would appear that a basic low-yield nuclear bomb would fill a void that does not need to be filled.

Earth-Penetrating Weapons

The second type, earth-penetrating weapons—known colloquially as "bunker-busters"—makes more sense but is still ultimately not compelling. Much of the public debate on these weapons has centered on relatively small versions and on whether they could be made fallout-free. They cannot be made fallout-free, as physics severely limits the distance they can penetrate into the earth.[12]

Instead, these weapons would be designed to increase their destructive depth, regardless of fallout. To increase destructive depth, the largest nuclear weapons in the American stockpile would be modified to penetrate the earth, roughly doubling the destructive reach of the most powerful weapons in the current arsenal. According to supporters of these weapons, this would help in two ways. First, it would better deter enemy leaders who might dearly value their bunkers (or more likely, the contents of their bunkers). Second, in extreme cases, if the United States knew that a WMD attack were about to originate from a deep underground bunker, it could destroy it with the new nuclear arms. This argument, however, runs into a problem: the proposed designs would improve the reach of U.S. nuclear weapons by a factor of two at best. If an enemy can avoid weapons in the current arsenal, it could without much more difficulty avoid the more powerful bombs by digging deeper underground, not much more challenging a task given the quality of modern tunnelling equipment (even older technology might get the job done).

The second argument for earth-penetrating weapons is that they could be used to reduce fallout when attacking underground targets. As a basic rule of thumb, one can reduce the yield of a weapon ten- to twentyfold while converting it into an earth penetrator and maintain the same destructive capability against underground targets.[13] This means that, all else being equal, an attack against an underground target with an earth-penetrating weapon could cause ten to twenty times less fallout than an attack on the same target with a bomb that did not penetrate the ground. That is not as useful, however, as it may sound. If the bomb is used far from an urban area, such a difference in the amount of fallout will not matter very much. If the bomb is used *in* an urban area, the fallout reduction is unlikely to matter much either, as most of the "extra" fallout eliminated would have fallen beyond populated areas anyhow; thus total casualties may not be significantly reduced. If a target is located in between these two zones, the earth-penetrator may make some difference, but only under this very specific and improbable set of circumstances.

Enhanced Radiation Weapons

Enhanced radiation weapons, the third option, are best known as "neutron bombs"—a technology debated and rejected during the 1980s. The purpose of such weapons is to kill enemies with radiation while preserving some of the nearby physical infrastructure. During the cold war, proponents of the neutron bomb argued with some credibility that it would be effective against massed Soviet armor, at the time considered the greatest threat to western security. But even then, hawkish opponents of the proposed bombs countered that precision-guided conventional munitions could do the job better.[14] Today, with precision-guided weaponry much more mature, there is no credible rationale for such a weapon.

Agent-Defeat Weapons

Agent-defeat weapons, are, from a military perspective, perhaps the most interesting. These weapons would be designed to penetrate facilities stockpiling chemical or biological weapons and incinerate them, thus preventing the spread of the deadly agents. But recent studies—including one by Michael May, former director of the Livermore National Laboratory—have questioned this claim.[15] They argue that without exquisite intelligence on the location of the facilities—of the kind the U.S. lacked in Iraq—an attack is unlikely to destroy the targeted agents. In some cases, chemical or biological agents might even be ejected into the air without first being neutralized by the heat of the bomb. Most important, conventional weapons—ranging from bleach-filled bombs to special incendiary weapons—show similar, if not sometimes greater, promise.[16]

On a related count, the United States must decide on its broader policy for using nuclear arms. American policy for responding to chemical or biological attack is intentionally ambiguous, even contradictory. The United States explicitly reserves to itself the right to respond with nuclear weapons, but it gives no indication of how it will actually decide to counterattack; at the same time, the United States has offered assurances for twenty-five years that it will not use nuclear weapons against a non-nuclear state unless the latter is allied with a nuclear power.

A policy that explicitly threatens a nuclear response would superficially be the most effective in deterring enemy use of chemical or biological arms. However, it would also be less than credible in many circumstances. Chemical and biological attacks might be scaled down (intentionally or unintentionally) to kill only tens or hundreds of people; a nuclear response would then be massively disproportionate, even using the low-yield nuclear weapons some propose. At the same time, there is no denying that for some massive biological attacks, a nuclear response would be proportionate. On balance, the current U.S. policy of strategic ambiguity is sound. However, the United States should emphasize its ability to retaliate conventionally over its nuclear capability, in particular given the greater credibility of the conventional threat. And it might further make clear that it would never be the first to use weapons of mass destruction in war.

The Comprehensive Test Ban Treaty

Given that it does not need new types of warheads, as discussed above, and that it can ensure the dependability of its nuclear deterrent without nuclear testing, as argued below, the United States could demonstrate its belief that nuclear arms are increasingly less valuable by ratifying the Comprehensive Test Ban Treaty. This is a controversial, if hardly new, recommendation. But the evidence argues in favor of the CTBT, and current opponents should reconsider their stance. If that does not happen and the CTBT remains unratified, the United States should at a minimum maintain its tacit compliance with that treaty by preserving its nuclear testing moratorium, for the good of its broader nuclear nonproliferation agenda.

Negotiated and signed in 1996, the Comprehensive Test Ban Treaty would ban all nuclear explosions by its member states or within their jurisdictions. Its twin goals are to prevent non-nuclear states from obtaining nuclear weapons and to prohibit nuclear weapons states from improving their arsenals, the latter point a condition attached to the indefinite extension of the NPT in 1995. If adhered to, the CTBT would do little to prevent countries from developing crude nuclear bombs (since testing is generally unnecessary for those) but it would complicate pursuit of fusion bombs or weapons small and light enough to be put on missiles. It could also bring the de facto nuclear weapons states, notably India, Israel, and Pakistan, under the broad umbrella of the global nonproliferation regime, should they choose to join. At the broad symbolic level, the CTBT would also reinforce the taboo not only against testing of nuclear weapons but also against their use. This taboo against nuclear weapons has been successfully leveraged in combating proliferation—for example, in arguing for confronting Saddam Hussein—making it important to reinforce.

To enter into force, the CTBT must be ratified by all states that are members of the United Nations Conference on Disarmament and that possess nuclear reactors, a total of forty-four states. The treaty would be supplemented by a global technical verification network, combined with procedures for on-site inspections.

In the United States, debate over the treaty has been highly politicized. In October 1999, the Senate rejected the treaty's ratification along partisan lines, by a vote of 51-48 (sixty-seven votes are needed for treaty ratification), after a bipartisan attempt to postpone its consideration.[17] A host of internationalist Republicans (including senators Lugar, Warner, Domenici, McCain, Hagel, Snowe, and Collins) opposed the treaty, with only four Republicans (senators Chafee, Jeffords, Smith, and Specter) supporting it. Among Democrats, only Senator Byrd failed to vote yes, and he voted "present" rather than no.[18] During the 2000 presidential campaign, Democratic candidate Al Gore promised to push for the treaty's ratification as a top priority, while Republican candidate and eventual winner George W. Bush rejected the treaty.[19] During the early months of the Bush presidency, administration officials investigated the legality of withdrawing the treaty from Senate consideration or even canceling the American signature on the treaty. Both efforts were shelved.

Treaty opponents followed four main lines of attack. First, they argued that the treaty endangered the safety and reliability of America's nuclear arsenal. By prohibiting explosive nuclear testing, they claimed, it would prevent weapons designers from verifying the effects of aging on the stockpile and thus from certifying its continuing viability. Second, they contended that the treaty was unverifiable—despite the extensive global monitoring network that the treaty proposed, they claimed, enemies could hide nuclear explosions in massive underground chambers, using a technique known as cavity decoupling. Third, they argued that states determined to test nuclear weapons would simply withdraw from the treaty or violate it openly—and thus that ratifying it would give America a false sense of security. Fourth, they argued that the CTBT would prevent the United States from developing new warhead types.

Each of these downsides is illusory or otherwise pales in comparison with the potential nonproliferation benefits of firmly opposing testing.[20] The Department of Energy's Stockpile Stewardship and Management Program (SSMP), a $6 billion-per-year effort to maintain and certify the stockpile's safety and reliability, promises to be effective into the foreseeable future. Moreover, if age-related problems were discovered in the stockpile, the United States could simply remanufacture the weapons to their original specifications.[21] (As a further hedge, it could also manufacture some simpler, albeit less efficient, weapons that would be virtually sure to work without testing.)[22] While remanufacturing weapons could cost slightly more than assessing the stockpile through testing, it would not be particularly expensive and would avoid contravening the test ban. The only case in which the United States would truly need to test is if it were to design and develop new nuclear weapons that have novel effects. As we argue above, however, the case for new types of warheads is weak.

Turning to the second argument, the ability of extremist states or other potential adversaries to cheat on the treaty is severely limited. First, hiding a nuclear test would be extremely difficult. If the yield of a weapon is made small enough to evade detection during a test, the test will not particularly be militarily useful. Thus even if compliance with the treaty cannot be *absolutely* verified, it can be *effectively* verified, since any important nuclear test will be detected.[23]

The third critique of the treaty—in effect, that it is unenforceable—is the most challenging. Indeed, treaty proponents have oversold its ability to prevent non-nuclear states from acquiring nuclear weapons. If a non-nuclear state were willing to violate the NPT, it could violate the CTBT as well. (That said, as of this writing North Korea has done the first but not the second.)

The CTBT's clearest direct effect would be to stop nuclear weapons states from adding significant capabilities to their arsenals. For example, analysts generally agree that China's adherence to the universal moratorium on nuclear testing has greatly complicated its pursuit of MIRVed warheads for its intercontinental ballistic missiles (ICBMs).[24] The CTBT might dissuade Russia from improving its tactical nuclear arsenal and integrating it further into its war-fighting strategy. Although such a goal is not of much direct military interest to the United States, it is valuable to help keep the nuclear threshold high. In contrast with rogue states that might openly violate treaties that they have signed, states like China and Russia would factor the international opprobrium associated with abrogating the CTBT much more heavily into their decisions about whether to conduct nuclear tests.

The process of ratifying the CTBT could also be used to help galvanize world opinion to confront proliferating states, particularly those states that attempt to pass the threshold of basic nuclear weapons. For example, while the great powers have failed to prevent North Korea from acquiring nuclear weapons, they may have deterred North Korea from openly testing weapons. The international moratorium on nuclear testing, now more than a decade old among the original five nuclear powers, has undoubtedly made it diplomatically more difficult for Pyongyang to test. DPRK leaders may well fear, for example, that testing would make it much easier for the United States to gain agreement among the region's main powers to impose economic sanctions on their country. This sort of dynamic admittedly already occurs without the CTBT in place; adding the CTBT would, however, help solidify it.

Safety of Strategic Nuclear Forces

One other straightforward arms control measure that could be undertaken to increase American safety would be to de-alert most U.S. and Russian strategic missile forces. During the cold war, Russia and the United States each believed that deterrence depended on the ability of each side to have a second-strike force. This led to efforts by each side to protect its forces. But it also tended to perpetuate "hair-trigger alert" postures, where very soon after receiving evidence suggesting an enemy launch, authorities would have to make an irrevocable decision of whether to retaliate by launching their own missiles.

Many analysts worry that such a high-alert posture dangerously increases the probability of nuclear war.[25] They argue that technical failures in early warning systems might result in false alarms leading to accidental war, as might poor decisionmaking by leaders under unnecessary time pressure. They point out that since the end of the cold war, Russia's early warning system has fallen into disrepair, creating an even greater probability of false alarms. They also point to the possibility of an unauthorized launch of Russian ICBMs, which they argue has been made more likely by "personnel reliability problems arising from the social and economic upheavals Russia has experienced over the past decade."[26] To remedy that, they consistently push for a reduced alert status for the U.S. and Russian nuclear arsenals.

Opponents have countered mainly by arguing that reducing alert status means increasing the chance that the enemy might believe that it can execute a successful first strike, thus weakening deterrence.[27] In addition, after the cold war, and particularly after U.S.-Russian relations significantly warmed beginning in 2001, some claimed that de-alerting was unnecessary, as neither side, in their estimation, would ever launch a nuclear attack. Further, they argued that de-alerting weapons would introduce an instability into the U.S.-Russian relationship: if either side *re-alerted* its weapons, it would be seen as an aggressive step by the other, even if the re-alert was not oriented toward it.[28] Some also have seen de-alerting as competing with national missile defense and have argued that a defensive shield offered better protection against unauthorized or accidental attack.[29] Last, opponents have contended that de-alerting by the Russians would be unverifiable.

Opponents of de-alerting are correct in their observation that U.S.-Russian relations almost entirely preclude the possibility of either side believing reports of an evolving attack and thus of retaliating. From that perspective, whatever the alert status and condition of the U.S. and Russian systems, the chance of attack will be nearly zero. This suggests that de-alerting, if pursued, should not be treated as a top U.S.-Russian priority. Cooperative threat reduction and other proliferation prevention programs should be higher priorities.

Still, America would on balance be more secure if Russia de-alerted its nuclear weapons. There is always a danger under present circumstances that an unauthorized launch could occur due to the rash behavior of a small number of individuals. Russia's high alert status requires frequent internal movement of warheads for maintenance, further increasing the chances of accident or theft. The decay of Russia's early warning infrastructure also presents a genuine problem, and unless comprehensive repairs are made and the system maintained, it could lead to false alarms. Any procedures that allow for a launch under inappropriate circumstances are dangerous—or at least, more dangerous than need be tolerated given the generally good state of U.S.-Russian relations—and should be revised if possible to reduce the chances of accidental nuclear attack. (This conclusion is unchanged by missile defense; no U.S. defense would be able to intercept more than a handful of Russian missiles for the foreseeable future.)[30] If verification were deemed necessary—we are not convinced that it would be—a de-alerting arrangement could be monitored reasonably well by allowing occasional short-notice inspections of ICBM silos and even, with somewhat greater difficulty, of ballistic missile submarines.[31]

Worries that a fully de-alerted force would weaken deterrence against third parties, such as rogue states, with which the United States still has confrontational relationships, should be taken seriously. Some have contended that prompt retaliation is not necessary for deterrence—only *certain* retaliation is—and thus that a fully de-alerted force is desirable.[32] While that may have been true vis-à-vis the Soviet Union and continues to be true against Russia, it may not be precisely the case against rogue powers wielding smaller numbers of weapons, who might use those weapons in a tactical fashion. In that case, prompt retaliation after an initial strike might dissuade the enemy from executing further strikes. Thus, any de-alerting should allow for rapid re-alerting of at least part of the U.S. arsenal. Since major crises typically develop over days and weeks, not minutes, that should not be difficult to achieve.

Some have suggested that in order to make de-alerting politically acceptable, only a fraction of U.S. and Russian weapons should be de-alerted.[33] That would greatly limit the benefit of this policy measure. But if partial de-alerting is all that Russia will accept, given a less-than-perfect verification scheme and the already reduced alert level of its submarine forces, it would be better than nothing. Partial de-alerting would at least reduce the number of places in its own nuclear forces where Russia would have to optimize safeguards and direct resources to prevent accidental or unauthorized launch. Although Russian concerns about first-strike vulnerability make little sense in today's world, they still persist in its bureaucracies (and in the United States too), so partial de-alerting may be all that is currently achievable.

Space

Space systems were a focus of arms control debate during the cold war, and many would still like outer space, the last physical frontier of the human experience, to be a sanctuary from military competition.[34] They favor binding, permanent, multilateral bans on space weaponry. Beyond their philosophical motivation, American opponents of the weaponization of space make a practical national-interest argument: as the world's principal space power today, the United States stands to lose the most from weaponization, since it could jeopardize the communications and reconnaissance systems on which the U.S. military and economy so disproportionately depend.[35] Opponents of weaponizing space also point to the world's growing economic dependence on space assets and to the risk of damaging those assets should weaponry be based in or used outside of the atmosphere. Non-American opponents of weaponizing space also worry about a unilateralist America pursuing its own military advantage at the expense of other countries, most of which do not favor putting weapons in space. This dispute has much of its origins and motivation in the history of the ballistic missile defense debate, as well as in the antisatellite weapons debate of the 1980s. But it has taken on a new tone in what many view as an era of American unipolarity or hegemony. In recent years, China and Russia have been consistent in their opposition to the weaponization of space and in their desire for a treaty banning the testing, deployment, and use of weapons in space.[36] So have a number of U.S. allies, including Canada, which proposed in 1998 that the United Nations convene a committee on outer space at the Conference on Disarmament in Geneva.[37] The United Nations General Assembly has also continued to pass resolutions, for more than twenty straight years, opposing the weaponization of space.

In contrast, developing more military applications for outer space is a priority for many American defense planners today. Much thinking about the so-called revolution in military affairs and transformation of defense emphasizes space capabilities. Ensuring American military dominance in the coming years—something proponents tend to see as critical for global stability as well as for unilateral advantage—will require the United States to remain well ahead of its potential adversaries technologically. For some defense futurists, the key requirement will be to control space, denying its effective use to U.S. adversaries while preserving the unfettered operation of American satellites that help make up a "reconnaissance-strike complex." Others favor an even more ambitious approach. Given that fixed bases on land and large assets such as ships are increasingly vulnerable to precision-strike weaponry and other enemy capabilities—or to the political opposition of allies such as Turkey, Saudi Arabia, and France, which have sometimes opposed use of their territories or air space for military operations (as in the recent war in Iraq and in the 1986 U.S. bombing of Libya)—they favor greater U.S. reliance on long-range strike systems. These include platforms in space.[38]

Advocates of space weaponry also argue that, in effect, space is already weaponized, at least in subtle ways. Most medium-range and long-range rockets capable of carrying nuclear weapons already constitute latent ASATs. Likewise, rockets and space-launch vehicles could probably be used to launch small homing satellites equipped with explosives and capable of approaching and destroying another satellite. Such capabilities may not even require testing, or at least not testing easily detectable from Earth. Advocates of weaponization further note that the United States is willing to use weapons to deny other countries wartime use of the atmosphere, the oceans, and land, raising the question of why space should be a sanctuary when these other realms are not. As Barry Watts put it, "Satellites may have owners and operators, but, in contrast to sailors, they do not have mothers."[39]

Specific military scenarios can bring these more abstract arguments into clearer focus. Consider just one possibility. If, in a future Taiwan Strait crisis, China could locate and target American aircraft carriers using satellite technology, the case for somehow countering those satellites through direct offensive action would be powerful. If jamming or other means of temporary disruption could not be shown to reliably interrupt China's satellite activities, outright destruction would probably be seriously proposed.

No space-based missile defense or antisatellite weapons (with the possible exception of an isolated experimental launcher or two) were deployed during the cold war. That did not, however, reflect any decision to keep space forever free from weaponry. Nor do existing arms control treaties ban such weapons. Instead, they ban the deployment or use of nuclear weapons in outer space, prevent colonization of heavenly bodies for military purposes, and protect the rights of countries to use space to verify arms control accords and to conduct peaceful activities.[40] In addition, in 2000 the United States and Russia agreed to notify each other of most space launches and ballistic missile tests in advance.[41] Most other matters are still unresolved. And the concept of space as a sanctuary will be increasingly difficult to defend or justify as the advanced targeting and communications capabilities of space systems are increasingly used to help deliver lethal ordnance on target.[42]

Some scholars do argue that the START I, Intermediate Nuclear Forces (INF), and multilateral Conventional Forces in Europe (CFE) treaties effectively ban the use of ASATs by one signatory of the treaties against any and all others, given the protection provided to satellite verification missions in the accords. But these treaties were signed before imaging satellites came into their own as targeting devices for tactical war-fighting purposes, raising the legal and political question of whether a satellite originally protected for one generally nonprovocative and stabilizing purpose can be guaranteed protection when used in a more competitive fashion. Moreover, no one argues that these treaties ban the development, testing, production, or deployment of ASATs (as opposed to their use).[43] Nor do any involve China.

The United States currently conducts few space-weapons activities, but that could change quickly. Many expected Bush administration secretary of defense Donald Rumsfeld to move in such a direction. Prior to entering office, Rumsfeld chaired a commission on the military uses of space, which warned that without taking a wide range of defensive and offensive steps, the United States risked a future "Space Pearl Harbor."[44] Indeed, as defense secretary, Mr. Rumsfeld issued a major strategic plan arguing that "the mission of space control is to ensure the freedom of action in space for the United States and its allies and, when directed, to deny such freedom of action to adversaries."[45] More concretely, the army has reportedly been working on laser dazzlers to blind surveillance satellites and jammers to disrupt communications and surveillance satellites, nondestructive technologies that make good sense.[46] It also has had a (now unfunded) kinetic energy ASAT program. Programs exploring other ASAT concepts were receiving funds as of mid-2004. Most notable is the NFIRE infrared satellite, primarily designed as a ballistic missile defense sensor but also potentially capable of executing hit-to-kill intercepts against objects in space.[47]

In this light, should the United States agree to restraints on future military uses of outer space, in particular the weaponization of outer space? Any useful formal treaties would have to be multilateral in scope. It makes little sense to consider bilateral treaties because it is unclear what country should be the other party to a treaty. At this point, any space treaty worth the effort to negotiate would have to include as many other space-faring countries as possible, ranging from Russia and the European powers to China, India, and Japan.

That accords would be multilateral does not mean that they should be negotiated at the UN, where many space arms control discussions have occurred to date. There is a strong and perhaps ideological pro–arms control bias in the UN Conference on Disarmament, where these discussions have taken place. In addition, some countries, such as China, may be using those forums to score political points against the United States rather than to genuinely pursue long-term accords for promoting international stability. The United Nations might ultimately be involved to bless any treaty, but it might be best to negotiate elsewhere.

First, however, one must decide whether any treaties are worth negotiating in the first place. Proposals for space arms control may be grouped into three broad categories. First are outright prohibitions of indefinite duration and broad scope. Second are confidence-building measures, such as requirements for advance notification of space launches and keep-out zones around deployed satellites. Third are informal understandings, worked out in talks or more likely established through the mutual actions of major powers.

Overall, space arms control should not be a top priority for the United States in the future, contrary to what many arms control traditionalists have concluded. Some specific accords of limited scope, such as a treaty banning collisions or explosions that would produce debris above a certain (low) altitude, and confidence-building measures such as keep-out zones near deployed satellites, do make sense. But the inability to verify compliance with more sweeping prohibitions, the inherent antisatellite capabilities of many missile defense systems, and the potential longer-term military need to counter efforts by other countries to use satellites to target American military assets all suggest that comprehensive accords banning the weaponization of space are both impractical and undesirable. That said, the United States should not help hasten the weaponization of space and indeed should work to avoid such an eventuality; it benefits from its own military uses of space greatly and disproportionately at present. It should take unilateral action, such as by declaring that it has no dedicated antisatellite weapons programs, to help buttress the current status quo as much and as long as possible.

Prohibitions

One type of arms control accord on activities in space would be quite comprehensive, calling for no testing, production, deployment, or use of ASATs of any kind, based in space or on the ground, at any time; no Earth-attack weapons stationed in space, ever; and formal, permanent treaties codifying these prohibitions. These provisions are in line with those in proposals made by the Chinese and Russian delegations to the UN Conference on Disarmament in Geneva. They also are supported by some traditional arms control proponents who argue that space should be a sanctuary from weaponization and that the Outer Space Treaty already strongly suggests as much.[48]

These proposals suffer from three main flaws. To begin, it is difficult to be sure that other countries' satellite payloads are not ASATs. This is especially true in regard to microsatellites, which are hard to track. Some have proposed inspections of all payloads going into orbit, but this would not prevent a "breakout," in which a country on the verge of war would simply refuse to continue to abide by the provisions. Since microsats can be tested for maneuverability without making them look like ASATs, it will be difficult to preclude this scenario. A similar problem arises with the idea of banning specific types of experimentation, such as outdoor experiments or flight testing.[49] A laser can be tested for beam strength and pointing accuracy as a ballistic missile defense device without being identified as an ASAT. A microsat can be tested for maneuverability as a scientific probe, even if its real purpose is different, since maneuvering microsats capable of colliding with other satellites may have no visible features clearly revealing their intended purpose. Bans on outdoor testing of declared ASAT devices would do little to impede their development or the actual testing of similar devices not explicitly weaponized.

Second, more broadly, it is not possible to prevent certain types of weapons designed for ballistic missile defense from being used as ASATs. This is partly a problem of verification. However, the issue is less of verification per se than of knowing the intent of the country building a given system—and ensuring that its intent never changes. The latter goals are unrealistic. Some systems designed for missile defense have inherent ASAT capabilities and will retain them regardless of what arms control prohibitions are developed, and countries possessing these systems will recognize their latent capabilities.[50] For example, the American midcourse missile defense system and the airborne laser would both have inherent capabilities against low Earth orbit (LEO) satellites, if given good information on a satellite's location—easy to obtain—and perhaps some software modifications. The United States could declare for the time being that it will not link these missile defense systems to satellite networks or give them the necessary communications and software capabilities to accept such data. But such restraints, while currently worthwhile as informal, nonbinding measures, cannot be easily verified and can be easily reversed. Thus no robust, long-term formal treaty regime should be based on them. Indeed, the problem goes beyond missile defense systems. Even the space shuttle, with its ability to maneuver and approach satellites in low Earth orbit, has inherent ASAT potential. So do any country's nuclear weapons deployed atop ballistic missiles. Explicit testing in ASAT modes can be prohibited, but any prohibition could have limited impact.

Third, it is not clear that the United States will benefit militarily from an ASAT ban forever. The scenario of a war in the Taiwan Strait is a good example of how, someday, the United States could be put at serious risk by another country's satellites.[51] That day is not near, and there are many other possible ways to deal with the worry in the near term besides developing destructive ASATs. But over time, a possible need for such a weapon cannot be ruled out.

There is a stronger argument for banning Earth-attack weapons based in space. Most such weapons would probably require considerable testing. That testing might well be observable, meaning bans could be verifiable. Furthermore, prohibitions on such weapons will cost the United States little, since it will retain other possible recourses to delivering weapons quickly over long distances (as may other countries). So a ban may make sense. The most powerful counterargument to banning ground-attack weapons in space is that the long-term need for them cannot be easily assessed now. But the above physical realities do suggest that the United States will be able to make do without them or to find alternatives.

A number of specific prohibitions, fairly narrowly construed, are worth considering as well. They could be carefully tailored so as not to preclude development of various capabilities in the future, given the realities and security requirements noted. But they nevertheless could help to reassure other countries about U.S. intentions at a time of still-unsettled great power relations and help protect space against the creation of excessive debris or other hazards to safe use over the longer term. Measures could include the following:

—temporary prohibitions, possibly renewable, on the development, testing, and deployment of ASATs or Earth-attack weapons or both

—bans on testing or deployment of ASATs above set altitudes in space

—bans on debris-producing ASATs.

Compliance with temporary formal treaty prohibitions would be no more verifiable than permanent bans. But they could make sense when future strategic and technological circumstances cannot easily be predicted.

There are downsides to signing accords from which one might very well withdraw, of course. If and when the United States could no longer support the prohibitions involved, it would likely suffer in the court of international public opinion by its unwillingness to extend the accord, even if the accord were specifically designed to be nonpermanent. The experience of the United States in withdrawing from the ABM Treaty suggests that the damage from such decisions can be limited. But that experience also suggests that it requires a great deal of effort to lay the diplomatic foundation for withdrawal, that bitterness about such a decision can persist thereafter, and that withdrawal from one treaty regime—however outdated—might be used as a justification by other states to withdraw from more important and less outdated treaties that they find undesirable. On balance, accords of indefinite duration should not be entered into unless one expects to remain part of them indefinitely.

Bans on testing or employing ASATs that produce debris make sense and could well be codified by binding international treaty. Destructive testing of weapons such as the Clinton administration's midcourse missile defense system or other hit-to-kill or explosive devices against objects in satellite orbital zones would not only increase the risks of an ASAT competition, it would also create debris in LEO regions that would remain in orbit indefinitely. (That is, unless the testing occurred in what are effectively the higher parts of the Earth's atmosphere, where air resistance would ultimately bring down debris and where few if any satellites fly in any case.) The U.S. military worries about this debris-producing effect of testing. To date, tests of the midcourse system have occurred at roughly 140 miles altitude, producing debris that de-orbits within roughly twenty minutes. Future tests will be higher. But a ceiling of 300 to 500 miles might be placed on such tests, and a ban placed on using targets that are in orbit.

Confidence-Building Measures

Another category of arms accords includes those that do not limit the weapons capabilities of states but instead seek to establish rules or guidelines for how states use their military assets. The goals would be to reduce tension, improve communications, and build safety mechanisms into how countries make military use of outer space. This arms control concept would build on some of the agreements that the nuclear superpowers signed to reduce the potential for unintentional nuclear confrontation during the cold war, including the 1972 Incidents at Sea Agreement and agreements to set up communications hotlines.[52] Here the stakes might not be so great, but they could still be great enough to justify some straightforward measures and rules of the road—as long as no great effort has to be expended to work out some commonly accepted practices.

One such idea is that of establishing keep-out zones around deployed satellites. There is no reason for a satellite to approach within a few tens of kilometers—or in some orbits within even hundreds of kilometers—of another satellite. Any close approach can thus be assumed to be hostile and ruled out as an acceptable peacetime action. States might consider formalizing this understanding of keep-out zones. The idea makes particularly good sense if there is a way to monitor compliance. Future American satellites are expected to have more sensors capable of surveying the environment around them, so this approach may work.[53]

What real strategic purpose would be served by such zones? Unless satellites were themselves given self-defense capabilities—making them difficult to distinguish from offensive ASATs—the zones could not be enforced. And any country wishing to develop a close-approach capability for the purpose of ultimately launching a large-scale ASAT surprise attack could develop that capability despite the existence of keep-out zones, by testing against its own space assets or even against empty points in space.

That said, the idea may still make sense, even though keep-out zones would not substantially limit military capabilities. First, creating such zones would add another step that any state planning an attack would have to address. ASATs could not easily be pre-deployed near other satellites without arousing suspicion (especially if the United States and other countries deployed satellites with sensors capable of monitoring their neighborhoods). Second, any state violating the keep-out zones would tend to tip off the targeted country about its likely intentions; conversely, respecting the zones would constitute a form of restraint that could calm nerves to some modest but perhaps worthwhile degree. And the United States has no need to place satellites near other countries' space assets in any case, so it would not be giving up anything to endorse such a rule of the road. On balance, this idea is a worthy one for a treaty regime, though not worth a great deal of top-level time to negotiate.

What of advance notice of space launches? Again, this type of accord, such as that reached between the United States and Russia during the Clinton administration, would not prevent a country from breaking out suddenly, nor would it place a meaningful constraint on capabilities. But as long as it was observed, countries would have additional reassurance that others were playing by the rules. They would also have time to prepare to observe the deployment of satellites from any launch, allowing slightly greater confidence that ASATs were not being deployed. As a peacetime rule of the road at least, it makes sense. Some have also suggested allowing international monitoring of space payloads prior to their launch.[54] This seems questionable, though, since satellites could be made into effective ASATs without carrying payloads that made that obvious.

On balance, most or all of these confidence-building measures are marginally useful. They will not prevent the United States from retaining its hedges against a future need for ASATs, whether in the form of dual-purpose ballistic missile defense programs or even dedicated antisatellite systems someday. They will not prevent China or another country from quietly building inherent ASAT capability either. But they will add an extra step or two that other countries choosing to weaponize space would need to deal with before threatening American interests.

Informal, Unilateral (but Possibly Reciprocated) Restraints

A final category of measures would not involve arms control at all—in the formal sense of signed treaties and binding commitments—but rather unofficial and unilateral restraints. Such restraints would not force the United States to tie one hand behind its back and leave other countries free to develop space weapons; rather, by adopting the restraints and thereby setting a precedent and a tone, the United States would aim to encourage other countries to reciprocate. To the extent others did not show restraint, the policy could be reconsidered. This approach has several precedents in international affairs. For example, during the first Bush administration the United States reduced the alert levels of some nuclear forces and took tactical nuclear weapons off naval vessels in part to encourage similar Soviet actions, which followed.[55]

This approach can work more quickly than formal arms control; it can also preserve flexibility should circumstances change. It is perhaps most useful when it is not absolutely critical that all countries immediately comply with a given set of rules or restraints. In other words, if the

United States would have ample time to change its policy in the event that other countries failed to cooperate, without doing harm to its security interests in the interim, there is much to be said for this approach.

Since the United States is not presently building or deploying space weapons, informal restraint would presumably apply to research and development and testing activities. As one example, if a treaty to accomplish this goal could not be quickly negotiated, the United States could make a unilateral pledge not to create space debris through testing of any ASAT.[56] The flexibility associated with such a pledge might permit it to go further and also pledge not to create any ASAT that would ever create debris, given that even if the United States needs a future ASAT, it would have alternative technological options.

The United States might also consider making a clear statement that it has no dedicated ASAT programs and no intention of initiating development or deployment of any. Accordingly, it should modify the existing NFIRE satellite program to drop development of its hit-to-kill intercept capabilities. It could also declare that it will not test any systems, including high-powered lasers, microsatellites, and ballistic missile defenses, in an ASAT mode. The latter approach would have the greatest chance of eliciting verifiable reciprocation by other countries.

The downsides to such statements are that if and when U.S. policy requirements changed, the statements would have to be repudiated, raising alarm abroad and risking a greater diplomatic problem than might occur if the United States had never held itself to informal restraints. The advantages are that they might buy the United States some time, allowing it to play its part in further stigmatizing space weapons it has no strategic interest in developing or seeing developed anytime soon.

Conclusion

Strategic nuclear arms control and missile defense limitations contributed in important ways to stabilizing the cold war military environment. In some cases, particularly in the nuclear offensive arena, they have some residual utility today. They can help protect Russia and America against accidental and unauthorized launch and can mildly reinforce the important message that nuclear weapons are not a particularly useful tool of state policy. In particular, the CTBT is sound, though even if it is not adopted, a continued moratorium on testing can achieve many of the same benefits. And in some new possible arenas of arms competition, strategic arms accords can be useful, such as a ban on the testing and use of debris-causing antisatellite weapons.

But most strategic arms accords should not be a major priority for future arms control. They generally regulate arms competitions that are no longer so dangerous. In some cases, compliance with them might not be verifiable, and in other cases they would be plainly undesirable. Simple, informal accords may occasionally be useful, as on U.S. and Russian offensive nuclear weapons; unilateral restraints sometimes make sense as well, as on antisatellite technologies in the current security environment. But developing more elaborate accords—on strategic nuclear offensive and defensive systems, on most classes of space weapons—and taking the time required to negotiate them are unwise. Devising them consumes enormous time and resources better left to addressing today's most pressing risk—proliferation of dangerous technologies to dangerous actors.

CHAPTER 3

Preventing Nuclear Proliferation

Despite stunning advances in science and technology over the past half-century, nuclear arms remain the most deadly proven weapons on Earth.[1] Perfect defense against nuclear attack is not technically feasible.[2] Meaningful mitigation of its consequences is all but impossible.[3] The overwhelming burden of dealing with nuclear weapons thus requires use of the full range of preventive tools.

During the cold war, nuclear arms control policy rightly focused principally on the U.S.-Soviet relationship, as evidenced in the approaches to arms control discussed in the previous chapter. But today, though both Russia and the United States still maintain thousands of nuclear weapons, there is little danger that either nation will use its weapons in a deliberate attack against the other. Instead, policymakers' primary worries are that terrorist groups or rogue states might acquire and use nuclear weapons or that a nuclear-armed state might use its nuclear status to shield terrorists on its soil or engage in regional aggression. Most of the arms control options discussed in chapter 2 are of little use in forestalling these new dangers.

At its most basic, American and international arms control strategy should be designed to stop the spread of nuclear arms—not to cap or to structure existing arsenals, but simply to prevent the possession of nuclear weapons by new actors. Current efforts are flawed in four principal ways:

the arrangements in use provide too little early warning of proliferation developments; the United States and the international community lack effective means for enforcing nuclear nonproliferation agreements and standards; the approaches employed do too little to provide compelling incentives for states to forgo nuclear arms; and the programs and policies in place do too little to stop terrorists, as opposed to states, from acquiring nuclear weapons.

To improve early detection of proliferation activities, all states should be required to accept tougher, broader inspections than are now the norm and to allow their weapons scientists to speak freely to inspectors under international protection. That requirement should be complemented by an agreement to constrain construction of sensitive dual-use nuclear fuel facilities—those for uranium enrichment and plutonium reprocessing—which can be converted to produce weapons-grade material far too quickly. Thus, if a state started to build a nuclear fuel facility, the world would have a strong chance of detecting it as a proliferation problem long before the program had progressed to the weapons stage, permitting a more effective response.

Means of enforcing compliance with requirements also need to be strengthened, and a major expansion of export controls, especially in places such as Pakistan, is necessary. (In the case of South Asia, for example, export controls should be a higher American priority than convincing Pakistan and India to sign the Nuclear Non-Proliferation Treaty or the Comprehensive Test Ban Treaty.) The coercive dimension of arms controls must also be extended, building on the Bush administration's Proliferation Security Initiative, under which inspections of suspicious ships in the coastal waters of participating countries already are conducted. Participants in the initiative should seek international authority for interdictions outside their territorial waters when there is reason for concern about a given carrier or ship. The United States and its allies should also agree to oppose acquisition of nuclear weapons with equal strength regardless of whether the state in question technically exits the NPT; they should then extend that agreement to bind all states through a Security Council resolution, if possible. States must attempt to agree in advance on when coercive instruments, ranging from interdiction to sanctions to force, should be used. Those instruments must not be used strictly as a last resort, but rather a necessary resort when all other options are unpromising.

No nonproliferation strategy will succeed, however, if it consists only of rules and punishments. It must also give states reason to comply voluntarily, largely to reduce the burden of enforcement by reducing the number of violators. In the past, the nonproliferation regime promised states bilateral U.S.-Soviet and eventual global nuclear disarmament, access to nuclear technology, and the prospect of non-nuclear neighborhoods in most parts of the world as key features of its incentive structure. But these incentives are no longer sufficient and are often ineffective. Any durable regime must recognize that states will seek nuclear weapons if they feel insecure without them and that any incentives that do not address that fact will be largely ineffective. We thus recommend that the United States and its allies offer to develop alliances and security guarantees with more countries—extending much of the NATO collective security logic well beyond Europe and other regions where the United States currently has strong security arrangements. Implementing this proposal would require major new American commitments and investments, but the proposal would be broadly consistent with American foreign policy of the entire post–World War II period and could be implemented gradually. It would complement the prospect of having non-nuclear neighbors as an effective inducement for states to refrain from developing or acquiring nuclear arms.

This would not preclude the use of nonaggression pledges as part of nonproliferation deals in difficult circumstances, as long as the deals were carefully construed not to reward proliferators or give them a blank check to carry out other threatening policies against their neighbors or their own citizens. (A case in point is North Korea.) Rather, it would complement such approaches by minimizing the number of problem cases that arise.

Finally, it is important to better secure existing nuclear materials. Increasing financial and political investment in the Nunn-Lugar Cooperative Threat Reduction (CTR) program—and aggressively expanding it well beyond the former Soviet Union—is necessary to secure nuclear materials and thus minimize the possibility of theft.

To prevent the deliberate transfer of weapons to terrorists, the United States should improve its ability to determine what country provided the material or weapon used in any future terrorist nuclear attack. There are technical reasons, discussed below, why this is more feasible than many assume. The United States should also declare a deterrent policy promising extremely severe repercussions for any country found to have exported weapons materials to others.

Securing and Containing State Nuclear Arsenals

Although terrorists are becoming more technically sophisticated, none can acquire nuclear weapons without taking advantage of an established state's technical base. In one scenario, a state might actively provide assistance—or even an assembled bomb—to a terrorist organization. In another, a state's weakness or negligence may lead to critical nuclear material being left unsecured, vulnerable to theft by a terrorist group. Policies that aim to prevent both of these possibilities are essential. It is also critical to prevent nuclear-capable states from aiding aspiring nuclear powers in their pursuit of weapons.[4]

Expediting Cooperative Threat Reduction

When the Soviet Union collapsed in 1991, American policymakers worried that its nuclear weapons might fall into the wrong hands. Russian officials had similar concerns but lacked the money to properly secure their stockpiles in the new, open environment. Recognizing a looming threat, senators Sam Nunn and Richard Lugar proposed having the United States fund the efforts of states of the former Soviet Union to destroy, consolidate, and secure their nuclear weapons, stockpiles of nuclear materials, and associated missile delivery systems.[5]

Originally envisioned as a means to help Russia implement its obligations under the START I Treaty, which required Russia to dismantle and destroy nuclear-armed missiles, the so-called Nunn-Lugar program and related efforts have since been expanded.[6] They now cover three main areas of activity: destroying unneeded weapons, consolidating and securing the remaining weapons and fissile materials, and re-employing former weapons scientists who might otherwise leave to work for rogue regimes. Program activities span the departments of defense, energy, and state and cost $1 billion in fiscal year 2003. In 2002, the G-8 leaders collectively pledged to spend $20 billion over the next ten years securing all weapons of mass destruction, not just nuclear weapons, in the former Soviet Union.[7] More recently, President Bush has sought authority to expand the programs beyond the former Soviet Union, arguing persuasively that inadequately secured bomb materials are found worldwide and thus need to be dealt with by a global regime.[8]

Work, however, is far from complete. According to a Harvard University study released in March 2003, only 17 percent of fissile material in the former Soviet Union has had a comprehensive security upgrade and only 37 percent has had even a basic upgrade.[9] Comprehensive upgrades have been done on only 10 percent of Russian warheads. Eighty percent of former weapons scientists have not found sustained civilian employment, raising the risk of a dangerous brain drain by countries or groups with an interest in nuclear weapons. And weapons-usable plutonium continues to be produced, despite no military need for it.

In the former Soviet Union, three primary obstacles stand in the way of more effective implementation of the Nunn-Lugar program. The most obvious is a lack of adequate funding. In 2001, the bipartisan Baker-Cutler Commission asserted the need to spend $30 billion over the following ten years to adequately address the problem. That is a somewhat high recommendation, assuming as it does no commercial value for surplus nuclear material.[10] Devoting roughly $20 billion for nuclear weapons alone might be appropriate, though given limited American knowledge of Russia's complete nuclear complex, flexibility is imperative. In any case, in 2003, only $1 billion was spent, and the U.S. government has no plans to significantly expand that amount in the near future.[11] The G-8 Global Partnership, which aims to enhance financial contributions from donors besides the United States, may increase that figure to $2 billion a year over ten years, though the funds will be spread across chemical and biological weapons as well as missiles and environmental cleanup. But right now, the sum of individual national appropriations falls far short of the $20 billion target.[12]

In the absence of new funding, the United States will need to better focus its efforts under the Nunn-Lugar program. It should concentrate primarily on Russia's nuclear weapons and materials stockpiles. While securing chemical weapons, radiological materials, and missiles is valuable, it should not be accorded the same priority. Within the realm of nuclear security, the greatest emphasis should be on conducting security upgrades, not on destroying warheads. Given an equal-cost choice between destroying already secured warheads or securing other, vulnerable warheads, the U.S. should pursue the second route. Stopping proliferation is more important than reducing the size of the Russian arsenal.

The second major problem is lack of access to sensitive Russian facilities.[13] Some of this is due to the excessive secrecy concerns of Russian bureaucrats and facility managers. That obstacle might be overcome by more frequent and forceful intervention by President Putin and his senior aides. Most likely, the United States will have to offer some level of reciprocal access to American facilities if it is to elicit the level of Russian cooperation necessary to make the Nunn-Lugar program work.

Third, Congress currently requires the president to certify that Russia is complying with all of its arms control obligations before any Nunn-Lugar CTR expenditures can be made by the Department of Defense in a given year. In a narrow sense, that might be prudent—for example, if Russia were producing new highly enriched uranium (HEU), the United States should halt funding for any program to eliminate existing Russian stores of highly enriched uranium. But it can have the perverse effect of holding successful nonproliferation programs hostage to marginally related and often less important arms control disputes. This is not the only impediment—other bureaucratic and political problems, such as those mentioned above, exist too. Nonetheless, congressional restrictions on the president's flexibility in spending CTR funds are a vestige of cold war U.S.-Soviet distrust, and repealing them could help speed cooperative nonproliferation efforts. The president should still withhold funding if Russia is taking actions that undercut the effectiveness of the program (as in the HEU example mentioned). But the United States should recognize the critical importance of threat reduction efforts, and not make funding for them hostage to most other matters in the U.S.-Russian relationship.

Expanding Cooperative Threat Reduction Programs

To be truly effective, cooperative threat reduction activities must extend significantly beyond the former Soviet Union. Besides the United States and Russia, at least six other states own nuclear weapons, and scores of others possess fissile materials in bomb-usable quantities.[14] While most civil facilities are covered by International Atomic Energy Agency (IAEA) safeguards, those safeguards are designed to deter unauthorized diversion by states party to the IAEA rather than to prevent deliberate theft. A new layer of protection to guard against theft or diversion by rogue elements is essential. Expanding CTR to states outside the former Soviet Union that do not possess nuclear weapons and that hold highly enriched uranium or plutonium at civil sites should be technically straightforward, provided sufficient funds.[15] One potential barrier is bureaucratic intransigence on the part of individual facility managers, like that which has plagued U.S.-Russian cooperation on civilian nuclear facilities. To address that problem, U.S. negotiators should be given broad authority to negotiate incentives tailored to individual facilities.[16]

Improving safeguards in states possessing nuclear weapons will present special challenges. The most straightforward cases are Britain and France, which are believed to have advanced, American-style security systems for their nuclear weapons.[17] China's rigid internal security apparatus and fairly stable domestic society likely provide significant protection against outsider theft and insider diversion of weapons or materials. But while aiding China to improve security measures presents several barriers, including legitimate U.S. concerns about potential Chinese espionage, doing so could have positive payoffs.[18] The United States should be concerned principally about sharing techniques for screening insiders, which, if properly understood by China, could aid in China's espionage efforts in the United States. For that reason, the United States may want to withhold cooperation on security methods involving personnel. Also, special precautions should be taken to prevent Chinese participants in bilateral exchange programs from using the programs as an opportunity for intelligence scouting. Nonetheless, sharing information on materials and warhead protection could be profitable: Chinese espionage within the American nuclear establishment, to the extent it has occurred, appears to have been directed at obtaining advanced warhead designs, not at stealing information about materials and warhead security techniques.[19] That is for good reason: China stands to gain little advantage over the United States by learning more about American techniques for securing nuclear warheads and materials. Thus useful assistance should be possible, even when working under constraints. Russia may also be able to provide China advice on ensuring the security of nuclear materials and weapons, drawing on what it has learned through the Nunn-Lugar program.

Cooperating with states outside the Nuclear Non-Proliferation Treaty that possess nuclear weapons but are not enemies of the United States—specifically India, Pakistan, and Israel—presents different, sometimes more significant, challenges. The Israeli case is perhaps the easiest to deal with, though it is nevertheless very delicate. Israel may not need any outside assistance, and that would be ideal, since it would prevent the United States from becoming more entangled in the Israeli nuclear weapons issue. But if Israel does need help, the close American-Israeli relationship should make both sides feel comfortable in sharing sensitive security technologies; certainly the United States should be comfortable sharing with

Israel any technology that it has been willing to share with Russia. Israel may be sensitive to any intimate cooperation, as it continues to publicly maintain that it does not possess nuclear weapons. U.S.-Russian cooperation on threat reduction, however, has never given the United States direct access to Russian warheads, suggesting that if similar assistance were needed, the United States could provide it to Israel. The only other danger in providing security assistance is that it might suggest that the United States condones Israel's possession of nuclear weapons. That would contradict stated American policy; it could also negatively affect America's image in the Middle East, as well as weaken nonproliferation norms. With these problems in mind, it would be wise to attempt to keep any nuclear security assistance to Israel secret and when possible deniable. At the same time, if assistance is also being provided to India and Pakistan, as we recommend below, the United States can honestly maintain to the world that it is not singling out Israel for special treatment in this respect.

Article I of the NPT obligates the five *de jure* nuclear weapons states not to "assist, encourage, or induce any non-nuclear weapon State to manufacture or otherwise acquire nuclear weapons or other nuclear explosive devices, or control over such weapons or explosive devices."[20] This may legally prohibit the United States from offering certain types of sophisticated assistance to India, Pakistan, or Israel, given that they are not formally recognized as nuclear weapons states by the NPT and indeed cannot be under the terms of that treaty. In particular, there has been considerable debate over the possible sharing of Permissive Action Links (PALs), electronic locking systems that prevent assembled nuclear weapons from being used by unauthorized persons.[21] Opponents of providing PAL and other technology to Pakistan and India (Israel is assumed to already have the technology) have noted, among other points, that such transfers would "assist" and "encourage" those countries in manufacturing fully assembled nuclear devices, in contravention of Article I. This is a debatable point. Providing security technology, no matter how intimately incorporated into nuclear weapon design, is unlikely to "assist" or "encourage" India or Pakistan to acquire *additional* nuclear weapons, though it might affect the way in which each state stores its weapons (intact or unassembled.) At the 2005 NPT Review Conference, the states party to the NPT should endorse this permissive interpretation.

The traditional concerns about accountability that have pervaded the U.S.-Russian CTR agenda—generally worries over whether recipients of assistance are using it for the stated purpose—will be even more difficult to address with India and Pakistan. There is little hope that the United States would gain access to sensitive facilities to verify that its security technology was being properly used. In the short term, given the absence of a clear solution to this problem, the United States should nonetheless begin to offer technical assistance without being able to verify that it is being properly applied. The risk of wasting a small amount of money is greatly offset by even a small probability of diminishing the nuclear threat, and security methods do not risk truly aiding India and Pakistan in the expansion or modernization of their arsenals.

In the longer term, new technology may be able, at least in part, to solve the accountability problem. Since the end of the cold war, America's nuclear weapons laboratories have devoted considerable energy and resources to developing and refining cooperative threat reduction technology. In particular, they have focused on so-called information barrier technologies, which provide the United States enough information to verify that Russian materials are secure without compromising the secrecy of sensitive Russian information.[22] At the same time, these technologies were designed so that their transfer would not give Russia any American security secrets. The labs ought to begin developing technologies that would address similar concerns about leaking sensitive information to Pakistan or India.

Still, the most contentious technology-sharing debate is over whether to aid India and Pakistan with PALs. Besides broader concerns about nonproliferation norms and the secrecy of American technology, several important objections to the transfer of PALs have been raised. Analysts worry that providing India and Pakistan with PALs could destabilize their relationship. Currently, both countries are believed to store their nuclear weapons with the fissile core separate from the rest of the weapon.[23] (It is believed, however, that Pakistan has deployed assembled weapons during crises over the past decade.)[24] Many believe that this is a stabilizing feature because it adds a step between the decision to use nuclear weapons and the actual employment of the weapons, allowing time for officials to reconsider and reverse their decision. However, since traditional PALs can be applied only to intact weapons, providing the technology would induce India and Pakistan to keep their weapons fully assembled. Early U.S. PAL-related technology, which was applied directly to weapon cores, could be used to avoid this problem in peacetime, were Pakistan and India to deploy weapons only during crises.[25] However, if the weapons were deployed in crisis, the PALs would then have to be deactivated, leaving the weapons again vulnerable to misuse. That is still far better than nothing, especially if Pakistan and India continue not to deploy weapons during peacetime. And since the United States should not want to encourage India or Pakistan to deploy intact weapons in peacetime (which, to be safe, would likely require more new nuclear testing to verify that the warheads would not detonate if dropped or otherwise mishandled), employing those types of PALs that are usable only on unassembled weapons is the extent of the responsible practical options currently available to Washington.[26]

While providing physical security assistance may be straightforward, assisting with personnel security, though challenging, may be more important. Policymakers must judge the danger to American security involved in describing how the United States screens sensitive personnel and compare it with the gains from sharing such information. In Pakistan in particular, where al Qaeda sympathizers have infiltrated security institutions, but also in India, the insider threat is extremely dangerous, suggesting that cooperation on personnel screening may be quite valuable. Assistance should begin only through conversations with a small group of highly trusted officials, and progress must be monitored carefully.

Pakistan presents another, unique, problem: if an internal regime change were to occur, its nuclear arsenal could come under the control of strongly anti-American leaders. Several authors have suggested the United States prepare for this possibility by developing military contingency plans to eliminate Pakistan's nuclear arsenal in a crisis.[27] But while appealing in its simplicity, such a plan would likely fail due to poor intelligence on the location of Pakistan's weapons. Instead, it might be wise to enter a dialogue with the Pakistani leadership as to how it might secure, or even destroy, its own weapons safely during a hostile takeover.

Should an international organization lead these cooperative threat reduction efforts? It would be unwise for the IAEA to aid states in securing their arsenals. If the IAEA were faced with the tasks of judging a state's compliance with the NPT and providing security assistance if the state were not in compliance, it would find itself in a difficult and counterproductive bind, with potential conflict of interest. If there appeared to be a need to expand the political base for cooperative threat reduction beyond the G-8 nations, a new international organization, not the IAEA, would best do the job. That would allow some states to contribute funds that they would be unwilling, for political reasons, to contribute to an explicitly American effort. It could also soften the diplomatic impact of assisting states in controversial situations.

Deterring States from Transferring Nuclear Weapons to Terrorists

Cooperative threat reduction can work when states share the international community's interest in keeping nuclear materials out of terrorist hands, but they may not always do so. The United States cannot be confident that some state will not want to *deliberately* transfer nuclear weapons to terrorists, a prospect that should be confronted by attempting to deter such transfers.

Nuclear weapons are difficult to detect; thus, rather than simply focusing on intercepting bombs, the United States must learn to identify a nuclear weapon's origin *after* it has exploded. There is no way to hide a nuclear attack. The challenge, instead of finding the bomb, would be to identify the bomb's origin from its residues. If the United States can take that technical step, it can credibly assure its enemies that their transfer of weapons to terrorists will ultimately lead to their own demise. Building on scientific techniques developed during the cold war, the United States stands a good chance of developing the tools needed to attribute terrorist nuclear attacks to their state sponsors. If it does, deterrence could become much more effective in controlling the spread of nuclear weapons.

Any nuclear explosion leaves behind traces from which the bomb's characteristics might be reconstructed, and scientists at the nation's three principal nuclear weapons laboratories are exploiting this phenomenon. They have decades of experience to build on.[28] According to a recent National Academy of Sciences study, "the technology for developing [an attribution] capability exists but needs to be assembled."[29] Before the testing of nuclear weapons in the atmosphere ceased, in 1963, the United States developed techniques to infer details of Soviet bombs by examining their fallout, which they could detect from far away. By positing a range of possible bomb designs, technicians could infer details about the fissile materials used in the Soviet bombs, along with some of the weapons' design details. (Presumably, the Soviets did the same to spy on America; thus the United States might cooperate with Russia to further develop its attribution abilities.) Some of that expertise is still maintained, particularly in conjunction with the Nuclear Emergency Search Teams (NEST), whose task is to respond to nuclear terrorist incidents. Building on that foundation will require training a new generation of scientists in forensic techniques long neglected. It will also require an effort by laboratory scientists to imagine weapon designs that terrorists or rogues might use. (The Department of Energy's Advanced Supercomputing Initiative could be used to simulate such designs, which would not require nuclear testing to validate.) It would be wise to pursue much of this in a (limited) multilateral environment, thus helping reassure the world that any attributions are sound and unbiased.

By itself, however, the ability to infer a bomb's composition will not be enough; to successfully attribute an attack, the United States must have a state fingerprint that matches it. To some degree, the United States can infer a weapon's characteristics from the design details of a state's production facilities and from the operating histories of its nuclear power and uranium enrichment and reprocessing plants. In other cases—like that of North Korea during the 1990s—special access to facilities will help to directly measure the composition of the enemy's uranium or plutonium. If the United States knows the isotopic details of the enemy's weapon, attributing it is much easier.

It may be possible to go further, by exploiting states' interest in not being wrongly identified as having originated a nuclear attack.[30] As part of an expanded role for the International Atomic Energy Agency, countries—including the United States—could be required to submit detailed isotopic data on the nuclear materials they produce (and submit to verification). If such states had good intentions, that would help exclude them from blame were a future terrorist attack to occur. So far, states have been loath to take such action, because sensitive military and economic data could be compromised. But their calculations could be different after an attack—a point that should be underscored now, to increase the deterrent benefits of the idea and thereby reduce the chances that any state will transfer dangerous weapons to a terrorist group in the first place.

New Rules of the Road for Civil Nuclear Programs

A viable arms control strategy also needs an improved means of preventing countries from using civilian nuclear programs—often developed with the help and blessing of the outside world—to develop nuclear weapons. This challenge was first illustrated clearly by India in 1974, when it appropriated supposedly "peaceful" nuclear power technology to build its first nuclear explosive. North Korea has followed this path as well. More recently, there have been persistent similar worries about Iran's nuclear program. Analysts have warned that if Iran were allowed to have and to operate nuclear reactors, it could then possess nuclear weapons within a matter of weeks—assuming that it had already built a clandestine reprocessing plant—allowing inadequate time for an effective international response.[31]

If there are to be credible options for enforcing nonproliferation, lines must be drawn before a country acquires nuclear weapons. We thus propose three new standards for international behavior. First, the production of highly enriched uranium should be indefinitely suspended everywhere. Second, an indefinite moratorium should be established on the construction of new nationally owned uranium enrichment facilities—which are designed to produce low enriched uranium (LEU) for nuclear power but can produce HEU for nuclear weapons as well. Any new plants would have multilateral ownership. (Full-scale uranium enrichment facilities are now located in ten countries—China, Russia, France, the United Kingdom, the United States, Pakistan, Germany, the Netherlands, Israel, and Japan. Iran owns a pilot-scale enrichment plant and a partly built full-scale plant; India has a small, 100-centrifuge plant. North Korea is pursuing uranium enrichment technology, but its state of development is unknown. Plutonium reprocessing facilities are known to exist in a similar group of countries, minus Iran, Germany, and the Netherlands but including India and North Korea.)[32] Third, an indefinite and worldwide moratorium on the construction of plutonium reprocessing facilities, which extract bomb-usable plutonium from used nuclear power plant fuel, should begin.

On HEU, an indefinite moratorium on the production of highly enriched uranium for civil purposes should be established. Existing facilities using HEU—research and isotope production facilities, test reactors, and critical assemblies—will be able to use replacement high-density LEU fuels within the next ten years.[33] They should be required to convert to such fuels as soon as possible. In the meantime, HEU supplies for the remaining facilities should be derived from excess U.S. and Russian weapons-origin fuel, as much of the LEU used in nuclear power plants is today. Further, exchange agreements should be developed to allow scientists from states without HEU-fueled research reactors access to reactors that are already operating. The production of HEU by states that do not currently possess it, then, would be regarded as evidence of intent to develop nuclear weapons.

Halting uranium enrichment would be another matter entirely. As long as nuclear power continues to be used, uranium enrichment will be required for fuel production.[34] And several plausible rationales, including resource scarcity, economic independence, and limiting carbon emissions, may support a state's decision to continue or even expand its use of nuclear power.[35] If new enrichment capacity is needed to fuel new plants, new enrichment facilities should be required to be under multinational ownership rather than being nationally owned or owned by a company under only a single state's jurisdiction.[36] (Placing *all* enrichment facilities under international control would be politically unrealistic as it would require governments to force existing owners of several commercial enterprises to sell a large fraction of their assets.) Lawrence Scheinman has noted that this proposal "appears to meet energy security concerns by providing participants with a legal and economic stake in the supply system, and to meet nonproliferation concerns by limiting the spread of sensitive facilities, localizing and complicating the risk of proliferation, and going beyond conventional verification safeguards."[37] Multinational ownership of facilities would also introduce a stronger nonproliferation safeguard because it would require states to appropriate property co-owned by foreign partners before converting it to illicit use.[38] That would hardly be impossible, but it would increase the odds of early detection of noncompliance. In addition, all owners would have to be states with long-standing records of compliance with the NPT. (This latter measure would be designed to prevent countries such as Libya, Iran, and North Korea—as well as Pakistan and indeed, at least for the foreseeable future, even India—from forming a consortium.)

The third standard—a ban on plutonium reprocessing—would treat most states that separate plutonium from used nuclear fuel as demonstrating intent to build nuclear weapons. In theory, this would be straightforward, since the preponderance of research indicates that once-through fuel cycles—those that directly dispose of nuclear waste without creating separated plutonium—are economically preferable to closed fuel cycles, which involve plutonium reprocessing.[39] Some argue that reprocessing is still needed to prevent accumulation of plutonium stocks that could someday be reprocessed and used in weapons. But as long as any reprocessing is under way, a state will always have a significant quantity of separated bomb-usable plutonium available, since the plutonium must be stored for some period before it is burned in a reactor and since even the reactor products contain plutonium. Shifting to reprocessing simply replaces a "plutonium mine" with a "plutonium river" that could be very quickly exploited to make weapons.[40]

However, several major industrial states—France, Japan, Britain, and Russia—persist with major reprocessing programs, and they are unlikely to terminate them.[41] (The United States is exploring reprocessing as well.) Continued operation of major reprocessing plants is not evidence that building new reprocessing facilities is economical, since their capital costs are already sunk. Further, continued operation of reprocessing programs by France, Britain, and Russia introduces no special ambiguity, since each of these states is a declared nuclear power. (Japan, of course, is not, but a single country with reprocessing capabilities and without a weapons program does not constitute a pattern of reprocessing, even if it is on balance undesirable.) However, new construction of reprocessing plants in Western states could suggest that reprocessing is economical and legitimate. To that end, Western states—including the United States—should not begin to build any new reprocessing plants. (The proposal should be restricted to *new* plants for the same reason given in the uranium enrichment case.)

These recommendations overlap in their purpose with several prominent recent proposals, including one made by President Bush[42] on February 11, 2004, and one by IAEA director general Mohamed ElBaradei[43] on several occasions around the same time. Their differences, however, are critical. President Bush proposed to restrict enrichment and reprocessing to states that already carry on those activities, while guaranteeing a fuel supply to all other states; ElBaradei proposed to allow all activities, but under multinational ownership. On the plutonium front, neither Bush nor ElBaradei was ambitious enough, since there is no legitimate reason for constructing new reprocessing plants anywhere. With regard to uranium enrichment, Bush probably asked for too much—a large number of states would likely reject his deal because it is highly discriminatory. Even if the United States attempts to establish such a regimen, it should expect no for an answer and propose alternatives. Meanwhile, ElBaradei asks both for too little, by suggesting no special requirements on the composition of any multinational consortiums, and for too much, by suggesting that the new rules be applied to all facilities, including those already in operation.

The above proposals also bear little resemblance to the often-advocated Fissile Material Cut-off Treaty (FMCT). The FMCT would require that fissile materials be produced for civilian use only, disallowing production for weapons use. The proposals outlined above would, in contrast, restrict a state's capacity to produce fissile materials in general, regardless of whether they were for civilian or military use. In essence, the FMCT would restrict the use of fissile materials, while our proposals would restrict their production. Under our proposals, the world could be given significant early warning of nuclear weapons development, as the arrangements would be violated as soon as states started improperly pursuing enrichment or reprocessing. In contrast, the FMCT would be violated only when a state labeled its plutonium "For Weapons" rather than "For Energy"—and the state could then have actual weapons within weeks.

How can agreement on new controls for nuclear technology be reached? Reopening the NPT to alter Article IV, which governs "peaceful" nuclear technology, seems as likely to lead to the NPT's collapse as to its strengthening and is thus best avoided. Instead, the United States should lead an effort to reinterpret Article IV, which is currently read as guaranteeing access to all nuclear technologies so long as states refrain from making nuclear weapons. At the 1995 NPT review conference, Article V of the NPT, guaranteeing all states access to so-called peaceful nuclear explosives, was collectively reinterpreted to deny states access to such devices, based on the twin observations that such devices were uneconomic and were problematic from a nonproliferation perspective. A similar effort could be made regarding Article IV.

The main barriers would be the lack of international consensus on which peaceful nuclear energy applications are economic and which are uneconomic, as well as on which are proliferation-prone and which are less so. To redress this disagreement, the United States might undertake an initiative similar to the International Fuel Cycle Evaluation (INFCE) program, which was started by the Carter administration and operated between 1978 and 1980.[44] In the wake of the 1974 Indian nuclear test, INFCE brought together technical analysts from forty-six countries and five international organizations to discuss the economics and vulnerability to proliferation of a host of peaceful nuclear technologies. INFCE brought about two highly valuable developments. First, it built some consensus on which nuclear activities were uneconomic, which in turn built greater consensus later on which technologies could be properly denied, Article IV of the Nuclear Non-Proliferation Treaty notwithstanding. Second, it provided a fairly noncontentious forum for delegate states to engage in productive discussions of appropriate nonproliferation policy.

In particular, according to various participants, it helped the United States persuade some (though far from all) countries of the essential correctness of its concern about the link between peaceful nuclear technology and proliferation.

Improving Assessment of Compliance

Agreements for controlling nuclear technology are worthless if those who enter into them do not comply. The first step in establishing compliance is ensuring the ability to monitor for violations. In some cases, that will be accomplished through formal verification arrangements provided for under the agreement; in others, it will be done in parallel to, but not as part of, the agreement, either unilaterally or in concert with others.

Expanding Inspections

Some monitoring can be done without the cooperation of the country in question.[45] Satellites and spy-aircraft can detect aboveground nuclear tests and in some cases can also detect state testing of conventional explosives whose blast configurations, in particular a spherical implosion arrangement, indicate nuclear weapons development. Satellites can also typically detect construction of nuclear reactors. Thermal imaging satellites can detect operation of major gaseous diffusion enrichment plants, which consume massive amounts of electricity. American-operated krypton-85 detectors can in some cases detect plutonium reprocessing activity if it occurs near international waters or in a state close to another state where the detectors can be positioned. And individual states can monitor exports of sensitive equipment.

But these types of methods offer no way to tell, for example, whether a uranium enrichment plant is being used to make low-enriched power plant fuel or highly enriched bomb-grade uranium. They typically cannot determine whether spent fuel is being diverted to extract plutonium for bombs. They are powerless to tell whether gas centrifuge enrichment facilities are being operated underground; they could even have trouble detecting underground nuclear power plants whose heat signatures were well camouflaged. Answering such questions requires the state being monitored to grant special access to its nuclear facilities and, in some cases, even wider access to hunt for clandestine sites. Why would a state do that? First, to prove to its neighbors and other interested states that it does not possess and is not developing nuclear weapons; second, to avert penalties other states might impose for its refusal to submit to such inspections; and third, to gain reciprocal access to inspect facilities of states about which it might harbor suspicions.

States party to the NPT are required to conclude "full-scope safeguards" agreements with the IAEA, under which the IAEA periodically monitors all nuclear facilities that the state under inspection declares. While these agreements provide for special inspections at suspected undeclared sites, inspections can be conducted only with the host state's permission, on a case-by-case basis, making detection of hidden facilities an unlikely prospect.

The international community realized this clear danger when, after the Gulf War, inspectors discovered a far more extensive Iraqi nuclear weapons program than they, or American intelligence, had previously imagined. In response, the IAEA developed the "93+2" program, under which states party to the Non-Proliferation Treaty are urged to adopt the so-called Additional Protocol to the NPT, developed between 1993 and 1997. Adoption of the Additional Protocol entails four principal commitments:[46]

—disclosure of a wide range of data regarding nuclear activities, including research and development and mining of uranium and thorium

—acceptance of IAEA inspections at any facility requested by the IAEA

—streamlining visa processing for IAEA inspectors to allow for prompt inspections

—affirming the right of the IAEA to use environmental sampling techniques, including wide-area sampling, to confirm the absence of undisclosed nuclear facilities.

In crafting the Additional Protocol, the states involved recognized that the United States, along with other nuclear weapons powers, could not submit to the full scope of its requirements, as doing so would expose those countries' nuclear weapons establishments to comprehensive inspections. Since it is unrealistic to expect nuclear weapons states to allow monitoring of their nuclear weapons design and production activities, the IAEA has an alternative framework under which they can accede to most, but not all, Additional Protocol obligations.

There is no guarantee that the technical means provided under the protocol will suffice to detect all illicit proliferation. The potential for developing covert gas centrifuge uranium enrichment facilities and plutonium reprocessing plants poses the greatest problem. In the future, laser enrichment facilities, which can be easily hidden, might become feasible for proliferators and thus of concern. But when combined with improved monitoring of nuclear-related commerce, tips from defectors, and other leads, Additional Protocol inspections can be very useful.

The IAEA should require all states under its safeguards to adopt the Additional Protocol, and it should refuse to certify a state as free of illicit activity if the state does not grant the IAEA the access it needs. That would be best pursued by making membership in the IAEA contingent on acceptance of the Additional Protocol. In this regard, the United States should lead by example and ratify its Additional Protocol agreement.

Enabling Whistle-blowers

These shortcomings suggest that the nonproliferation regime needs to better exploit not only technical but also human resources, and it needs not just more resources, but better ones. To address that issue, it must consider how to encourage more high-quality "whistle-blowers" from countries with secret and illicit nuclear programs to come forward.[47] As a first step, the United States could provide a valuable incentive to any scientist whistle-blowers from any suspect regime who might provide important information by according them and their families a standing right to protection, while providing disincentives to dissuade those who might give fraudulent information. Ideally, the initiative would be expanded internationally and closely integrated with the existing nonproliferation regime.

Scientists are unlikely to defect and inform if they believe that either they or their families will be targeted in retribution by the regimes they plan to betray. But perversely, scientists fleeing states where they would be persecuted for exposing illicit weapons programs have ambiguous status as refugees under international law. The United Nations High Commission for Refugees excludes from protection any person who "has been guilty of acts contrary to the purposes and principles of the United Nations"—and participation in an illegal, clandestine WMD program would likely fall in that category.[48] At best, scientists could not be confident that they would find protection outside their home country, and that uncertainty would unnecessarily deter them from defecting.

In principle, there is a simple unilateral solution: make a standing offer of American sanctuary and witness protection to any scientists with evidence of a clandestine WMD program who are willing to defect and testify against their former state.[49] But there are challenges. Consider, for example, a hypothetical scientist who defects and claims protection under the new American plan. He testifies that a certain facility, which he can identify on a map, is being used to produce weapons-grade anthrax. In this hypothetical scenario, American authorities would immediately have to answer a tough question: How credible does the defector's account have to be for him to be granted protection? One approach would place the burden on the defector—unless his claim could be verified, he would not be given protection. This approach would likely work with claims about large, fixed facilities that have no legitimate alternative uses, such as plutonium reprocessing plants and undeclared uranium enrichment centrifuge cascades.[50] In those cases, there are international legal mechanisms for conducting special inspections and thus for confirming accusations. Moreover, it would be difficult for a state to cleanly decommission and dismantle such a facility before inspections could be conducted.

Revelations about smaller or dual-use facilities could prove problematic, however. Defectors with information might fear that by the time authorities were able to inspect a suspect facility, it might be dismantled or scrubbed clean, leaving them unprotected and open to retribution from their home government. To address that concern, America could instead assume the burden of proof itself: unless the defector's claim could be disproved, he would be given protection. This approach would reassure any honest whistle-blowers that they would be protected and would thus be more effective in inducing defections. Unfortunately, it could also backfire. Scientists seeking U.S. residency might make false accusations, betting that their claims would never be verified as either true or false—as, for example, it appears that some dissidents affiliated with the Iraqi National Congress did in the years before the 2003 war in Iraq. Unless carefully structured, such an approach might lead to a glut of abuse, discrediting the asylum system and ultimately leading to its demise.

One promising way to address this dilemma would begin with the enactment of legislation providing asylum for whistle-blowers from any state at any time, with the burden of proof resting on the whistle-blower—and significant criminal penalties for anyone later found to have lied. But the legislation would also contain a provision allowing the president to designate specific states as being of urgent concern with respect to proliferation. Scientists defecting from those states and claiming to have information on illicit weapons activities would be presumed to be telling the truth; only if they could be shown to be lying would the United States strip them of special protection. Having such a system in place in advance would allow for quick activation. Such an arrangement could have been useful during the inspections in Iraq, for example, where it was urgently needed; in that case, harboring a few extra untruthful Iraqi scientists would have been considered a small price to pay for drawing out more valuable defectors. Today, the special designation and protections might be applied to Iranian and North Korean scientists.

This new American initiative should be considered only a part of a broader initiative to offer asylum to whistle-blowers that would include the international community. If too many scientists and their large extended families have to be absorbed, Americans may tire of the system. Moreover, the plan might come to be seen as an extension of American intelligence gathering rather than as a component of the global nonproliferation regime. That, in turn, would hamper effective use of defector testimony by international institutions such as the International Atomic Energy Agency or future UNSCOM-like inspection teams. And, at a more abstract level, expanding the sphere of states offering whistle-blower protection will help reinforce and extend international norms against the proliferation of WMD.

To begin, the United States should press friendly governments to enact national legislation similar to the American legislation proposed above. But to gain greater legitimacy, the United States should attempt to embed the whistle-blower initiative in international law. It could seek a Security Council resolution affirming that scientists who are willing to report illegal WMD programs can claim status as refugees, notwithstanding the statutes currently excluding them explicitly from such protection.

Slowing Proliferation

Rather than attempting to end proliferation outright, many useful nonproliferation tools seek instead to slow its progress, allowing time for other tools to be brought to bear on the problem. Export controls typically have been the key way of buying time for other nonproliferation tactics, such as regional peace agreements or a change of regime within a country considering the acquisition of weapons of mass destruction. They have been supplemented recently by the Proliferation Security Initiative, essentially a coercive form of export and import control.

Expanding Export Controls

Controls on nuclear exports have been a part of international security systems since nuclear weapons were first developed. Moreover, for most of that period, the controls have been multilateral, in the sense that mutually supportive controls have been implemented in different states. In the past three decades, those controls have become more formalized, with the Nuclear Suppliers Group (NSG) coordinating a broad multilateral export control regime. The NSG, which initially involved seven states, began in 1974, in the immediate aftermath of India's first nuclear test. By 1978, the group had expanded to fifteen states, and it aimed its efforts at harmonizing regulations on exports of sensitive nuclear technology.[51] The NSG's regulations are publicly promulgated through the IAEA, though they are not formally binding on the group's members.

The effectiveness of export controls has decreased consistently during the past two decades.[52] (India acquired nuclear weapons before the advance of multilateral export control regimes.) Most significant, as the cold war ended, many countries with different perceptions of the international security environment became members of various export control regimes. Because these regimes operate on a consensus basis, the United States often fails in its attempts to tighten controls on recipient countries of the greatest concern.[53] (The most prominent example of this has been Russia's continuing civil nuclear sales to Iran, which Russia did not regard as a state of proliferation concern. This is a subtle problem, which might have been avoided by focusing on restricting transfers of fuel-cycle technology while allowing reactor sales to proceed.) Extremist states have also become progressively more adept at concealing their procurement attempts, using businesses as fronts and shipping materials through nonsuspect states.

States outside the traditional export control cartels have also emerged as secondary suppliers of nuclear weapons–related technologies. Pakistan was found to have transferred gas centrifuge enrichment technology to North Korea, an action that led directly to the crisis that began in late 2002.[54] In the past it aided Libya's and Iran's centrifuge programs as well.[55] North Korea has been and continues to be an active vendor of ballistic missile technology, and many worry that it will expand its activities to include sales of nuclear-related technology.

Even before the emergence of secondary suppliers, it was very difficult to make export controls work well. With the likes of Pakistan and North

Korea now potentially involved as merchants, any effort whose goal is an airtight export control system could well fail. Even so, reforms should be pursued with the goal of tightening the system and *slowing* development of nuclear weapons programs, thus allowing time for inducements and coercion to thwart proliferation. Five lines of attack make sense:

—First, the United States should enhance information sharing with its export control partners, as recommended in 2002 by the GAO.[56] As part of that, it should also improve information sharing with international organizations like the IAEA and Interpol, as recommended in the February 11, 2004, speech by President Bush. It is difficult to be more specific about what this sharing of (classified) information should entail, but in general, other countries will be inclined to tighten their controls only if given intelligence highlighting critical threats.

—Second, no additional states should be admitted to the NSG—and thus given the ability to block NSG consensus—until they demonstrate that their perception of security risk is similar to that of the regime's central (primarily G-8) members. This is an important inducement, as NSG membership makes importing sensitive technology easier.

—Third, if consensus is possible within the NSG, the United States should press for a halt to uranium enrichment and plutonium reprocessing–related exports, as proposed by President Bush on February 11, 2004, in order to partially enforce stricter rules for access to such sensitive fuel-cycle components.

—Fourth, the United States should explore the possibility of forging a legally, rather than politically, binding NSG regime that includes penalties for noncompliance. This would create a more consistent regime. It should also advocate majority rather than consensus decisionmaking.[57]

—Fifth, Pakistan's export controls require special attention. On one hand, at least some transfers of sensitive nuclear technology from Pakistan may not have been condoned by the Pakistani government, meaning that effective Pakistani export controls might have thwarted them. On the other hand, high-level Pakistani authorities may have been complicit in several devastating transfers of technology, meaning that anything they learn about export controls might be used to help other states evade NSG controls. The United States must balance these two competing effects of cooperating on export controls. For the time being, the United States should assist Pakistan with implementing only basic export controls, erring on the side of not passing too much detail about American methods. Taking a lesson from the U.S.-Russian experience, the United States should first focus on making sure that Pakistan's legal and administrative systems are properly configured to catch and deter undesirable exports.

Coercive Export Controls: The Proliferation Security Initiative

The Proliferation Security Initiative (PSI), announced by the Bush administration in May 2003, began as an effort to work with a relatively small group of allies to intercept shipments of WMD-related materials to or from extremist states. The initiative, which essentially imposes coercive export controls on states that do not cooperate with WMD export control regimes, leverages international norms against the spread of weapons of mass destruction to gain support for its actions. (According to some participants, the PSI also seeks to cut off illicit export revenues, for example, from illicit drug sales, to states of concern. This aspect of it has more in common with sanctions than with export controls.) Contrary to some suggestions, the PSI would have a very limited chance of detecting transfers of fissile materials, but it could be used to thwart sales of bulky equipment for producing weapons or weapon materials.[58] Therefore it could be used to slow development of nuclear weapon and other WMD programs and to deter would-be customers, who would face a greater probability of being unmasked. It provides an important example of how arms control standards can be effectively mated with more coercive tools of security policy.

The PSI was initially restricted to interdicting shipments in the territorial waters of any one of its member states, which originally included Australia, France, Germany, Italy, Japan, the Netherlands, Poland, Portugal, Spain, the United Kingdom, and the United States. In March 2004, Canada, Norway, and Singapore joined the core group, and in June 2004, Russia joined as well. Most initial effort was directed at developing methods for sharing actionable intelligence in a timely fashion, securing approval for states to conduct interdictions in other states' waters, and sharing techniques for inspecting ships. Little was discussed about expanding the initiative, or, in particular, about obtaining new legal authority to conduct interdictions in international waters. The idea was to minimize the bureaucratization of the initiative; indeed, one of PSI's strengths is that it relies on the domestic laws and individual initiatives of participating countries rather than on formal international procedures for deciding on action.[59] It is a very good model for one important future type of arms control.

U.S. authorities were rightly cautious about including additional states in the initiative. They were wary of the problems that have confronted an expanded NSG, which has difficulty obtaining consensus on which states pose a proliferation concern. If, however, states can reach agreement on that issue, expanding the PSI would make sense. And certainly any countries wishing to pursue the spirit of the PSI by inspecting ships in their own coastal waters should be encouraged to do so. Some sixty nations have expressed support for the initiative, so such an outcome is possible.[60]

The United States would also be wise to seek international authority to interdict shipments in international waters.[61] As it stands, shippers can in theory evade the PSI by traveling only in friendly or international waters and by avoiding ships registered in countries that participate in PSI. (Liberia and Panama have joined, meaning that now ships accounting for about 30 percent of the world's cargo trade are covered by the regime and can be boarded even in international waters.)[62] Further expanding interdictions to the high seas would remove that option. To be sure, if the United States knew for certain that a given ship or aircraft was carrying highly enriched uranium or plutonium to or from an extremist state, it would, if nothing else were possible, simply stop it, justifying the action as self-defense under Article 51 of the UN charter. But circumstances are seldom so straightforward, and even in unambiguous circumstances it would be politically useful to have additional cover. What if hostile vessels avoid the territorial waters of U.S. allies and it is not clear which ones are carrying dangerous materials?

The United States needs a legal rationale for boarding ships from states of proliferation concern while they are on the high seas and for using force, if necessary, to do so. It also needs a way to prevent the uncontrolled overflight of aircraft from the same countries, even if it has only strong but not incontrovertible evidence of dangerous cargoes. The United States could argue that countries with highly oppressive internal policies, a history of attacking their neighbors, or demonstrated recent sponsorship of terrorism merit special attention for possible nonproliferation violations. A Security Council resolution could declare that, by behaving in such a way, a state would lose much of its sovereign right to protection. Once the Security Council subsequently declared that a specific state fell under the resolution, authority for searches of its international cargoes would be automatic. This would not always work—for example, China would be very reluctant to designate North Korea a target, at least right now—but it would still be a useful tool under some circumstances.

Inducing Compliance

The United States and its allies must be careful about offering economic or energy incentives to try to persuade other countries to comply with nonproliferation standards. Such incentives have a role in nonproliferation strategy, but they must not be seen by would-be proliferators as the predominant reason for forgoing dangerous weapons. The two bargains of the Nuclear Non-Proliferation Treaty—Article IV, giving non-nuclear states access to peaceful nuclear technology, and Article VI, committing nuclear weapons states to good-faith disarmament negotiations—have, unfortunately, reinforced the perception in some quarters that nonproliferation is not a good in and of itself. Worse, to the extent that states see refraining from developing nuclear weapons as being contingent on American, Russian, and other disarmament efforts, the nonproliferation regime will be excessively held hostage to American and Russian disarmament, which can only proceed so far in the coming decades.

Efforts to induce states whose programs are not driven by security concerns to comply with new arms control standards—for example, persuading Brazil not to build reprocessing or enrichment facilities—can make good use of economic tools. In the case of Brazil, for instance, avoidance of building reprocessing facilities would set a good example by demonstrating that Brazil recognized the option to be uneconomical, and international compensation for dismantling any technology already procured could ameliorate the financial penalty of compliance. As a general rule, states whose nuclear technology pursuits are economically motivated will be amenable to economic inducements, but such tools will rarely be decisive with states whose primary concern is security.

For states that feel insecure and might therefore consider acquiring nuclear weapons, the United States and its allies should consider steps that would ameliorate those concerns directly.[63] In the past, perhaps the most successful approach to this challenge has been the U.S. commitment to ensuring collective security through NATO and other security partnerships. Collective security arrangements appear to have had a positive effect in restraining proliferation. Aside from France, no nation of continental Europe has acquired nuclear weapons. Other American allies, such as South Korea and Taiwan, felt secure enough that, after flirting with nuclear weapons, they refrained from developing them.

Extending collective security, as discussed in chapter 1, should be a key pillar of a new arms control strategy. The United States and its allies should offer to create new security guarantees and perhaps new alliances tailored to specific circumstances for democratic, peaceful countries, and in some cases, for states that fall somewhat short of that description.[64] These would have to be broad and public assurances, promising U.S. and other allied assistance in repelling any unprovoked external assault on a country's territorial integrity. More limited security assurances like those offered to Ukraine when it gave up its nuclear weapons may sometimes be adequate. The United States, the United Kingdom, and Russia promised not to attack Ukraine and further pledged to seek immediate U.N. Security Council action to assist Ukraine if it ever were attacked.[65]

While this expanding collective security community may include states with ambivalent attitudes toward the United States, it would not of course be extended to include American enemies such as North Korea or Iran. Still, security guarantees may be placed on the table in negotiations with such states. In particular, security arrangements like those offered to Ukraine should be considered. The distinction in these cases is that in exchange for a security assurance, these states must do more than adhere to nuclear nonproliferation standards; their other problematic behavior (North Korea threatening South Korea as well as huge numbers of its own people, Iran sponsoring terrorism) must be addressed for sweeping security guarantees to be appropriate.

Ultimately, however, the states responsible for upholding the nonproliferation regime must be willing to acknowledge that security guarantees and other inducements may prove to be insufficient or inappropriate. In some cases, coercive tactics—discussed in chapter 5—will be necessary.

CHAPTER 4

Controlling the New Technologies

While nuclear weapons remain the most dangerous technological legacy of the twentieth century, many have speculated that emerging technologies could rival or even exceed the horrors of the atomic bomb. Advanced biological pathogens that spread easily and resist treatment, nanotechnology devices claimed to have the potential for uncontrollable self-replication, and computer attacks capable of bringing down huge segments of the world's electronic—and thus physical—infrastructure, are all notable entries on the list of potential twenty-first-century threats. Certainly, if the worst fears were confirmed, some of these threats would rival the lethal power of the atom. Are these fears accurate—or at least plausible? And can arms control—cooperative efforts by a group of countries to constrain dangerous technologies—mitigate or reduce the dangers?

This chapter focuses primarily on the biological threat, because it is both the most immediate and the most serious and because it is where arms control is likely to be most relevant in the years ahead. Moreover, tools developed to address it may ultimately help to supervise, monitor, and perhaps control the development of nanotechnology, although the case for controlling nanotechnology is not yet compelling. Cyberthreats are fundamentally different. They are less hypothetical than the threats posed by nanotechnology, but they are more amenable to being addressed by strictly defensive measures—and they are even harder to address through arms control techniques.

Treaty-based arms control is of limited use in dealing with the next generation of biological threats, but deterrence, defensive technologies, and homeland security measures will be critical. Approaches like the 1972 Biological Weapons Convention have been weakened because advances in microbiology make weapons technologies much easier to obtain, and the fact that biological agents can be produced in remote, hidden places on a small scale means that treaty-based control regimes relying heavily on international inspection are not particularly promising.

But if arms control were defined more broadly to include the coordinated use of domestic legislation by individual countries to restrict and monitor biological research activities, it would have more potential. It might not be able to prevent the willful efforts of extremist countries to acquire dangerous weapons, but it could reduce the risk that terrorists would obtain them as well as the risk that advanced pathogens would quickly spread if they were developed. Some traditional arms control transparency and oversight measures can be a useful adjunct to the coordinated national legislation approach, but they cannot be the core of national policy.

Biological Threats

Biological agents have the potential to equal nuclear arms as the world's most menacing weapon of mass destruction. Advances in microbiology and improvements in genetics may be extraordinarily promising for medical purposes, yet deeply worrisome for national security, potentially producing pathogens that are both highly lethal and highly contagious and against which no vaccines or treatments currently exist. In addition, laboratories that can be used to work on biological weapons abound. They can be very small and hard to detect, and they are easily disguised as legitimate research facilities.[1]

Consideration has been given in recent times to adding intrusive monitoring provisions to the Biological Weapons Convention (BWC). The BWC already bans the production, stockpiling, and use of biological arms, but compliance is not currently verifiable. However, while the right verification protocol to the BWC could be helpful, it would not be sufficient, because it is implausible that any such protocol would ensure the reliable detection of illicit activity. Also insufficient though also worthwhile (but outside the scope of this book) is the idea of building up American and international public health infrastructure to enable early diagnosis and treatment of any illnesses resulting from an attack.[2]

Meanwhile, the microbiological threat is growing. Already, for example, researchers have learned how to transform a virus like smallpox so that it can also suppress the host's immune system.[3] They also are closer to the day when an easily spread virus like influenza might be joined to an extremely lethal virus like smallpox to create a new type of virus with the contagiousness of the former and the latter's devastating effects. Alternatively, the smallpox virus might be combined with a pathogen like the Marburg virus, which is less contagious and slower acting but which causes a hemorrhagic fever for which there is no known cure.[4] Or genes controlling the production of substances that destroy common antibiotics could be spliced onto a relatively common pathogen such as anthrax. (For example, beta-lactamase, which destroys penicillin, could be spliced onto anthrax; although penicillin is no longer the drug of choice for dealing with anthrax, similar techniques might be used to counter drugs like ciprofloxacin.)[5] States might hesitate to use such agents, which could easily come back to infect their own citizens. But a state possessing an antidote or vaccine—or an apocalyptic terrorist group—might not care about the risk. Not all of these dangers may materialize, but none can be dismissed as of this writing, and some are more likely than unlikely.

With traditional arms control not up to the task, how can the dangers of advanced biological pathogens be minimized? It is tempting to think that a sweeping measure to classify advanced biological research might prevent the development and spread of such agents. It cannot. Even if the world were prepared to surrender many of the health benefits it derives from the open exchange of advanced biological information, too much information and too many advanced research techniques are already widely known. In addition, the paths to developing weapons are far more diverse than in the nuclear field. It often is hard to know in advance which lines of research will produce results that the United States and its allies would not want rogue states or terrorists to have access to, and important information will inevitably slip through any plausible classification scheme and into the public domain. Classification may sometimes slow this process and thus is often a sensible approach to controlling access to specific genes or pathogens.[6] But it is not a robust barrier to proliferation. Moreover, only about half of all major biological research is now done in the United States, and it will be feasible to do an increasing amount in small overseas laboratories as science progresses.[7] Besides, the sheer number of people involved in biological research around the world, in many different countries, makes closing off a large fraction of biological researchers impractical.[8]

Still, weaponizing biological agents—preparing them in ways that enable them to kill thousands, rather than tens, of people—is not easy. Developing advanced pathogens may actually be quite hard, at least given current technology.[9] True, over time, creation of these types of threats is likely to come more and more within the reach of terrorist groups. But slowing the spread of know-how and technology and the development of advanced pathogens is itself a worthy goal. If, over time, defenses against biological attack improve or the overall strength of terrorist movements can be reduced, an arms control strategy that for now simply slows the acquisition of dangerous pathogens could dramatically reduce the risk of biological terrorism.

Addressing the threat of biological terrorism requires a combination of better domestic law, better intelligence, stronger coordination of international legal approaches, greater support for Nunn-Lugar and related efforts in the former Soviet states, and greater research into defenses, including vaccines and medical treatments.[10] It is not a case of choosing between traditional arms control options and other approaches to address the problem; all are needed, and several are discussed below. That said, the right arms control tools must be selected if effort is not to be wasted on largely useless procedures that might create an aura of effectiveness without preventing proliferation. And the United States and its allies must avoid arms control concepts that could impair biodefense efforts. For example, using the wrong type of verification mechanism could provide an ill-intentioned government with an entrée into the biodefense efforts of a country that it intended to threaten with advanced pathogens. Several specific arms control tools are discussed below.

A Better Monitoring Protocol to the Biological Weapons Convention

A detailed verification protocol was proposed in 2001 to give teeth to the Biological Weapons Convention, which bans the production, possession, and use of biological agents but has no verification or monitoring mechanism whatsoever. Given that the treaty has been violated at least three times by signatories (the Soviet Union, South Africa, and Iraq), the argument for some type of monitoring system appears to be strong.[11]

The verification protocol rejected by the United States in 2001 had several features in common with the "challenge inspection" procedures of treaties like START, the Conventional Forces in Europe (CFE) Treaty, and the Chemical Weapons Convention. The protocol allowed challenge inspections—inspections that could be carried out with just twelve hours' notice—at sites where illicit weapons might be hidden. But it also incorporated means to control access to sites and to protect the types of proprietary secrets that are found at many pharmaceutical plants and research laboratories.

The basic concepts of the proposed protocol were, first, that major biological research and production facilities were to be declared, and second, that routine visits were to be allowed, up to 120 a year worldwide, divided among states party to the Biological Weapons Convention so that all parties would be required to allow some visits but none would be required to accept too many. Two weeks' notice was to be allocated for each visit. In addition, suspect-site or challenge inspections were to be authorized for other sites, based on evidence of suspicious activity deemed credible by the administrative body of the protocol. Access could be managed by the visited party so as to protect proprietary and national security information, assuming that it could satisfy the questions and interests of the inspectors in other ways (a big assumption, especially given the small size of biological materials). Confidentiality rules were envisioned to protect proprietary secrets, no samples were to be allowed to be removed from inspected premises, and inspected countries were to be given some right to vet inspectors.

The Bush administration opposed the proposed protocol, deliberately undermining a negotiating forum known as the Ad Hoc Group that had been working on a verification system since 1995. The administration was convinced that the group was blind to the flaws of the proposed verification protocol and thus unlikely to produce a better concept in the future. The administration initially wished to terminate the effort and undertake negotiations only on less formal types of multilateral biological technology controls, but it ultimately agreed to a series of short annual meetings leading up to a more substantial review in 2006.[12] Those meetings are to focus on coordinating national mechanisms for controlling access to dangerous biological technologies and on strengthening international mechanisms for monitoring any use of biological pathogens as well as responding to any such misuse that may occur.[13]

The Bush administration rightly recognized that the envisioned inspections might not reliably find many illicit weapons programs—and might perhaps find none. It may also have feared that American biological defense programs, which were pursued by both the Clinton and Bush administrations, might conduct various types of investigations and tests that brushed up against the treaty's prohibitions. (For example, the U.S. military was investigating variants of anthrax and building devices that simulated what Russian biological weapons bombs might have done—activities that are permissible under the BWC but too close to the line for the U.S. government to have wanted aired publicly.)[14] A final and even more powerful worry was that inspections might be used by bad actors to learn the microbiological details of specific medicines that the United States was developing and thus circumvent U.S. biodefenses.

The same sort of worry arises from the possibility of theft of physical samples that have commercial potential. Addressing concerns about theft requires a biological weapons inspection regimen that excludes inspectors from countries suspected of violations, allows inspected countries limited veto rights over who enters their territory, and makes it as difficult as possible for individual investigators to acquire physical specimens while doing their jobs.

The Bush administration also argued that any verification protocol would create a presumption that parties that appeared to be in good standing should be granted access to biological technologies (as suggested in Article 14 of the proposed protocol, which calls for "facilitating free trade and the fullest possible exchange in biological agents, toxins, equipment and materials"). This could have the effect of weakening an export control consortium known as the Australia Group, which presently includes most major biotechnology suppliers. In other words, according to the administration, the United States would have to trade existing tighter controls on dangerous technologies for the limited benefits of inspections.[15]

If these problems cannot be resolved, the U.S. administration would be right to oppose a BWC verification protocol. It would risk recreating the types of problems the world has recently been experiencing with the Nuclear Non-Proliferation Treaty, which in some ways actually helped potential proliferators to develop illicit weapons and provided cover and legitimacy for their activities.

There were ways in 2001 to make the proposed BWC protocol acceptable and useful to the United States, but the administration may not have considered them negotiable. For example, the United States could have insisted on unanimous consent of those currently trading responsibly in biological materials before allowing any new country into the trading group. And it could have made clear that it intended to keep out any countries that did not fully comply over a period of time with all arms control obligations or that were aggressive toward neighbors or involved in international terrorism. This approach would have required modification or reinterpretation of the existing BWC, which requires only that countries comply with its stipulations in order to be eligible for "peaceful commerce" in biological technologies.[16] Again, it might or might not have been negotiable. But in the future, the United States could negotiate while stating its preparedness to walk away from a verification system that does not accomplish those goals.

The Bush administration's position—which rejected even the *possibility* of a satisfactory agreement—was on balance regrettable, but the issue is complex enough that its view was not entirely unreasonable. The BWC verification protocol that the administration rejected did not propose the right inspection system, and the administration was substantively right to oppose it, although the way it did so was diplomatically wrong. In particular, it was wrong not to work to create an alternative approach.

A Multilateral Biosecurity Strategy—Coordinated, Toughened Domestic Policies

In recent years the United States has tightened restrictions on biological materials. In 1996, Congress passed the Anti-Terrorism and Effective Death Penalty Act, requiring among other things that all shipments of hazardous microbial pathogens and toxins to be registered with the Centers for Disease Control and Prevention (CDC). In the fall of 2001, the Patriot Act was passed. Among its other stipulations, it prohibited possession of dangerous biological materials without good research or medical reasons, and it restricted any exchange of these materials with individuals from countries on the State Department's terrorism list. In 2002, President Bush signed the Public Health Security and Bioterrorism Preparedness and Response Act, requiring entities working with any of thirty-nine select agents to register with the CDC and implement safety and security measures, including background checks for employees. This act also authorized the Animal and Plant Health Inspection Service to adopt similar safeguards for pathogens that could affect animal health or plant products.[17] All of these measures were appropriate—and overdue.

Other Western countries are taking similar steps, though not all are as far along as the United States. The Australia Group exchanges information so that transfers denied by one country do not (in theory) occur later through a different supplier. But many countries, Western and non-Western, do not yet have adequate domestic laws or controls. And the international export control system is highly imperfect, involving as it does only thirty-three supplier states with various types of domestic regulation.[18]

The United States should seek, through coordination of efforts rather than a multilateral treaty, to bring as much of the rest of the world as possible up to the safety and security standards that it has adopted in recent years. Countries unable to meet these standards or disinclined to work hard to adopt them would be prevented, when possible, from gaining access to the most advanced research technologies or to higher education programs and conferences for their scientists.

The Bush administration promoted a similar international scheme after September 11, 2001, but with too little focus and vigor. For such an approach to succeed, member countries should establish national registries of dangerous materials and their locations, require surveillance and security measures at the relevant sites, perform background checks on employees, create a paper trail for all transactions involving technologies and pathogens of interest, and impose bans on biological trading with dangerous countries, groups, and individuals. They should also create an international advisory body to which any member state could turn for further advice or assistance with these matters.[19] They should promptly and systematically share information with each other on exports that are denied by one country—as noted, a requirement of the Australia Group but not always respected—and continue to update their national legislation to keep up with future modifications and improvements to security standards.[20] The United States and its allies should also provide technical advice and possibly financial assistance for the initial regulatory and legal reforms that less advanced participating states will need to undertake to meet these goals.

International Monitoring of Research

Some have advocated creating an international oversight board to monitor the most dangerous types of otherwise legitimate research activities.

The goal would be to ensure transparency and peer review among as many institutions as possible throughout the world, except those suspected of illicit activities or in countries suspected of illicit activities. This system would not necessarily directly detect a laboratory dedicated to malevolent purposes, particularly if it were state sponsored. But enough information could be collated about every country's network of scientists and research institutes to make it easier to detect those attempting to evade notice. The omission of known scientists from various databases could tip off curious eyes, and whistle-blowers might be more inclined to reveal activities they knew to be wholly illegal. While it would be no panacea and would have limited power, such a system should be seriously considered.

This approach was first proposed by Elisa Harris and John Steinbruner of the University of Maryland. Their proposed Biological Research Security System would involve three levels of possible peer review. The first two would be domestic. A Local Pathogens Research Committee, similar in spirit to existing mechanisms for monitoring activities such as human clinical trials of new drugs, would monitor and in some cases approve projects that involved potentially dangerous research activities. More dangerous work would be monitored by a National Pathogens Research Authority in each participating country, focusing on controlled agents already known to be dangerous. This national board would also monitor and license members of the local boards, in the United States and elsewhere.

Finally, a global body, known as the International Pathogens Research Agency (IPRA), would be created to monitor the most sensitive research. Its approach would bear some similarity to the World Health Organization's approach to smallpox, and, as implied by the name, its membership and scope would be international. (An analogous effort in a different realm of technology is the 1994 Convention on Nuclear Safety, which encourages and facilitates adoption of safe standards for civilian nuclear power plants.)[21] The IPRA's domain would extend to research on the most dangerous controlled agents, such as smallpox; it would also adjudicate which particular research activities fell under the scrutiny of each monitoring panel.[22]

An approach along the lines of that proposed by Harris and Steinbruner would be voluntary and would rely principally, though not exclusively, on national efforts. Any implementation would have to be carefully tailored not to disallow research into defenses against dangerous pathogens; if it did not allow such defensive efforts in states in good compliance with their BWC obligations, it would do more harm than good. But that problem should be resolvable.

While initially voluntary, the overall approach could develop teeth over time. Countries refusing to participate in the system, not complying with their obligations, or credibly suspected of hiding illicit activities could be excluded, to the extent technically practical, from trade in biological materials and the growth media needed to work with such materials. If the situation were sufficiently serious, they could also be pressured in other, broader ways going beyond the immediate realm of the biological sciences. Ultimately, though, the system would not be a reliable tool in stopping countries from conducting illicit activities, since it involves no inspection team with independent resources and the right to demand access to hidden or suspect facilities. And even if joined with a verification protocol to the BWC, it would not reliably detect or stop all illicit activities.

Better Defenses

Arms control will never be a perfect tool for preventing the proliferation of dangerous biological agents, given the nature of the agents and technologies involved. Like other types of arms control described in this book, therefore, biological controls should be viewed as complements to—not substitutes for—other control mechanisms ranging from military force (discussed in chapter 5) to defensive measures.

Defenses are very important in the biological sphere. Soon after the 2001 anthrax attacks the federal government quickly increased funding for research into new vaccines and antibiotics and other medications as well as resources for purchasing and stockpiling certain kinds of antidotes. Such efforts had begun under President Clinton, but they rapidly accelerated after the September 11 and anthrax attacks. The specifics of which medications to develop and purchase and when will always require expert judgment that balances risks and costs, but the overall approach is sensible. However, research into broad direct defenses against possible future agents is also needed.

What does broad, direct defense mean, when one does not know what type of pathogen to design a defense against? Homeland security efforts, including measures such as installing improved air filtration systems in large buildings and public facilities, have a role. But they will not suffice, and they are not practical in all settings. For that reason, physiologically based defenses are needed as well.

Stanford University's Christopher Chyba and Alex Greninger have offered the most comprehensive proposal to date.[23] They argue that it is hard to know in advance whether physiologically based defenses will be feasible against the types of agents that may be created in the future. Direct defense would try to protect people against all plausible genetic mutations of various existing agents like bubonic plague, anthrax, and smallpox. In theory, that could prove impossible, given the sheer potential of any organism for random mutation, as constantly occurs with the common flu virus. In practice, however, only some mutations or modifications may prove especially stable and lethal, and there may arrive a point at which further mutation renders a pathogen too weak to be very potent or dangerous. Chyba and Greninger argue that although it is too soon to know, it is quite plausible that in such a hypothetical case the defensive agent could dominate at least some types of pathogens, because the offensive-defensive "arms race"—or mutation-antidote race—would reach a termination point rather than continuing endlessly. As a result, the importance of defense should not be underestimated.[24] This approach could also give a further boost to efforts to improve international public health monitoring of disease outbreaks, since ideally research on defenses also would take account of mutations and new diseases that arise naturally. But part of the virtue of this concept is that, to a large extent, it could be pursued even without the cooperation of all countries.

Enforcement

The combination of measures advocated earlier for dealing with nuclear proliferation—transparency, early warning, tighter limits on related commercial technology, and timely international response to any violations—is less promising for dealing with biological technology. Some of the ideas mentioned earlier, such as protecting whistle-blowers, combined with those developed above, such as revamping the monitoring protocol for the Biological Weapons Convention, would help. But while such measures may be necessary, they are unlikely to provide sufficient foundation for a universally successful arms control strategy.

These observations lead to several conclusions. First, as noted, developing biological defenses to the extent technology allows is critical. Second, since development of increasingly virulent biological pathogens is likely to spread in the twenty-first century, a deterrent of last resort is needed to prevent their use by state or state-sponsored actors. The United

States and its allies should not develop biological weapons of their own, given their existing arms control commitments and the difficulty of controlling the effects of biological arms. But they do need an effective and robust deterrent against use of biological weapons by state or state-sponsored actors and particularly against a catastrophic attack using advanced pathogens. Nuclear weapons can play this role in extreme circumstances. The United States technically has forsworn this option for nearly three decades by issuing "negative security assurances" to non-nuclear countries indicating that they would never be subject to an American nuclear strike unless they were allied in war with a nuclear state. It is doubtful, however, that any state has been fully confident that, in an extreme situation, the United States would not resort to a nuclear response. Indeed, while such security assurances make general sense, they need to be coupled with some ambiguity in cases where an enemy could execute an extremely devastating attack, perhaps one as lethal as a nuclear strike. In this respect, the first Bush administration had it right in its dealings with Iraq prior to Operation Desert Storm in 1991, when it sought to worry Iraqi leaders that a biological attack might be met with an unconstrained American response of some kind, possible nuclear.

For most plausible circumstances on the horizon, the United States and its allies could probably respond to a state-sponsored biological attack with conventional means only. Moreover, the threat of regime change will usually be at least as powerful as the threat of nuclear retaliation.[25] But the United States must also consider scenarios that, however unlikely, cannot be entirely dismissed—such as those in which a conventional response would be too slow to prevent further biological attacks while a nuclear response would take effect more quickly.

Deterrence will, of course, be more effective against state and state-sponsored actors than against autonomous terrorist groups. The United States and its allies may not be able to prevent terrorist groups from gaining access to first-generation biological weapons, such as powdered anthrax. Nevertheless, in addition to taking homeland security precautions and developing biodefenses, they should try—for example, by keeping al Qaeda on the run and depriving it of sanctuary. And by holding states accountable for more advanced programs, they can use deterrence to limit the threat posed by more advanced pathogens into the foreseeable future.

Third, despite all of the associated difficulties, special inspection regimes like those imposed on Iraq after Operation Desert Storm should be considered again in the most difficult cases, accompanied by the threat of strong coercive measures including military force to ensure access and improve the odds of compliance. Such inspection systems require remarkable access, and even then they are not completely effective. Iraq did not relinquish all of its biological programs for years, even when such inspections took place. But over time, the inspection regime made it much harder for Iraq to maintain biological weapons programs with ease and impunity.[26] It will require special circumstances for such programs to be considered again, but such circumstances could arise.

Fourth, more coercive enforcement tools, including military force, should never be taken off the table. Advanced biological weapons in particular can be every bit as dangerous as nuclear weapons, and the dangers associated with them will only increase over time. In the next chapter we consider a host of options in detail. They should all be on the table if evidence of serious biological weapons programs is uncovered in extremist states, whether or not they are parties to the Biological Weapons Convention.

Nanotechnology

The problems presented by biotechnology and nanotechnology—the latter the area of technology dealing with artificial objects with dimensions on the order of billionths of a meter—are similar. Some argue that nanotechnology devices could be given the ability to self-replicate without limit, enabling them to consume large fractions of the world's atmosphere, oceans, or other key elements.[27] Or they might, like bacteria, attack the human body from within.

Whether this doomsday scenario is at all plausible remains a subject of impassioned debate. Some treat it as a real possibility; others dismiss it as either extremely far off or simply impossible. Alternatively, some assume that proper ethical standards and arms control treaties can be devised to help prevent the catastrophic possibilities of nanotechnology.[28] A common argument against the possibility of developing massively destructive nanotechnology is that living small creatures capable of self-replication have enormously complex genetic codes that would be very hard to mimic artificially.[29] Another line of argument contends that designing devices that could mechanically assemble atoms into replicas of themselves requires far too clever a machine, with far more finesse in handling chemicals, than is realistically within grasp.[30] In general, these arguments focus on what is realistic in the near term, not on what might eventually be possible. And small, self-propagating organisms—bacteria and viruses—do of course exist, and some propagate extremely well, suggesting that there may be no prohibitive limits on nanodevices (although there may well be practical engineering constraints). To the best current understanding, then, artificial creatures with similar characteristics cannot be ruled out in the longer term.

If nanotechnology threats do materialize, they may pose challenges similar to those of microbiological threats. Thus the mechanisms discussed above for monitoring research in advanced biological agents might be used, at some future point, to manage nanotechnology. A code of ethics could also be established, and again international bodies could be used to coordinate and strengthen member countries' domestic laws in order to monitor nanotechnology purportedly being investigated for peaceful purposes. Transparency and peer review regimes could be devised to make these ideas concrete.[31]

Neither the current scientific state of nanotechnology nor what is now known about its risks justifies such measures. Studies of the question are needed, though, and the scientific community should be encouraged to examine the issue more thoroughly, but resolution of the matter is likely to be a long way off.[32] The biotechnology issue lacks such ambiguity, and it should be the priority for international monitoring and coordinated domestic controls. Once that has been addressed, there will be time to assess whether nanotechnology can and should be confronted too.

Cyberthreats and Cybersecurity

Computer technology has expanded enormously, as has its role in everyday life and in the management of public and private infrastructure. Given the prevalence of computers and the Internet, massively violent means are not needed to threaten important elements of national economic life and the basic functioning of society. Computer viruses and hacking have become insidious threats of great concern. In the words of a recent National Academy of Sciences study:

> How do potential cyberdisasters compare with disasters in the physical world? As the catastrophic events of September 11, 2001, demonstrate, disasters in the physical world can involve massive loss of life and damage to physical infrastructure over a very short

> period of time. The damage from most cyberattacks is unlikely to be manifested in such a manner—although interference with medical information systems and devices could affect lives. If undertaken by themselves, cyberattacks could compromise systems and networks in ways that could render communications and electric power distribution difficult or impossible, disrupt transportation and shipping, disable financial transactions, and result in the theft of large amounts of money . . . additional harm can come from the interactions of cyber and physical systems under attack that endanger human life directly and affect physical safety and well-being. . . . For example, a successful cyberattack launched on the air traffic control system in coordination with airliner hijackings could result in a much more catastrophic disaster scenario than was seen on September 11, 2001.[33]

How serious is this threat, and what can be done about it? What if anything can arms control do to reduce society's vulnerability to disruptions of its key electronic and computer assets?

The above assessment suggests that cybersecurity needs to be viewed in terms of tiers. First are systems that are so critical to national security and so important for sustaining human life that they must be made as robust as possible. Second are systems that are very important to the country's economy, even if they are less likely to cause physical harm when attacked and disabled. Third are systems whose disruption could cause considerable personal inconvenience and perhaps even economic loss to some or many individuals but would present little threat to society as a whole. Vigilance needs to be greatest for first-tier threats.

In all cases, the problem with computer technology and the Internet in particular is that large capital resources are not needed to wreak havoc. The world's worst computer bugs have been hatched by individuals in both affluent and developing countries. Placing barriers in their way through some sort of international arms control arrangement would be next to impossible.

That said, the world can live with individual hackers. Occasional hacking or bug-infestation are not of particular national security concern; rather, experts fear a coordinated computer attack that may also involve physical attacks on certain infrastructure. That means that the greatest threats are from countries that willfully encourage development of computer bugs and viruses. In other words, just as there is a tiered system of

U.S. computer systems to protect, some more critical than others, there is a range of threats, from the inconvenient and relatively benign to the much more serious and capable.

A Role for Arms Control?

Given the cybersecurity situation—a diffuse threat, the huge technological difficulty of preventing cyberattacks outright, the serious but containable consequences of computer attacks—the antidote is probably not a formal type of technology control regime. There is no known practical way, short of dismantling the Internet, to physically "control armaments" in this domain. There are methods for improving defenses, discussed below. But directly controlling the technological means of attack is unrealistic.

There is still a role for formal, multilateral government action. As with controls on biological pathogens, however, it has more to do with coordinating responses at the domestic level than with creating supranational authorities with intrusive powers of investigation and punishment. Countries should enact severe criminal penalties for hackers, bug-writers, and spammers. As a matter of state policy, they should discourage such nefarious computer activity by private individuals, and they should exchange information as quickly as possible on any threats they discover, from within or outside their own territory. (However, information on third-party threats should typically be shared only among like-minded states. For example, if the United States discovered that a computer virus originated in India, it might not share information about its origin with a country encouraging hacking as a matter of state policy—though it presumably would share information on any threats coming from its own territory with all parties.)

The above discussion pertains to the current cybersecurity environment. But if a threat someday involved a major attack against major infrastructure or very large numbers of private users, sterner responses could be appropriate. The basic logic guiding retaliation should be simple, clear, and publicly advertised, though not formally codified; the international community makes no distinction between deaths caused by cyberattack and deaths caused in any other malicious way.

These kinds of measures are not what many view as classic arms control. They are closer to law enforcement, with the potential for using diplomatic pressure and perhaps even penalties such as economic sanctions against countries that willfully tolerate or even support aggressive computer attacks.

Defensive Measures

There are several other ways in which the United States and other countries can improve protective measures against cyberthreats, not by reducing the offensive potential of attackers so much as by mitigating the harm that the attacks might cause. In that respect, they are in the realm of defense rather than arms control. These measures range from sharing information on threats more quickly, to improving the nation's cadre of individuals specializing in computer security, to developing stronger national standards for cybersecurity, vigorously promoting them, and encouraging the private sector to adopt them. In addition, there are specific measures that the U.S. military should take to ensure the robustness of its information systems against attempts to attack or breach them.

Several industry groups share information on cyberthreats among companies within their industry, but efforts at national information sharing have not been as successful, the government's Y2K clearinghouse being an exception.[34] The government can take several steps to encourage private sector cybersecurity information sharing through a central clearinghouse. First, all voluntarily shared information should be exempted from the Freedom of Information Act (FOIA) and all disseminated information should lack identification of its source (or have "hashed" identification of the source, allowing the source to reveal its identity later if desired). Second, a central clearinghouse should assume responsibility for mapping network interdependencies and testing information security systems throughout the nation, as proposed by the Hart-Rudman Commission on National Security/21st Century. To ensure the sharing of the most important information, the government should mandate the reporting of security breaches that could threaten critical societal functions.

The government should also share intelligence on cyberthreats and coordinate procedures for investigating international cyberattacks with friendly countries. As one manifestation of this approach, it and its close allies should create a multilateral clearinghouse to map vulnerabilities and interdependencies. Another priority is improving cybersecurity in the government's own information technology systems, including the networks that store and share nonclassified information.[35] These measures would have a dual purpose—protecting important government information and providing the private sector with an example of the best practices for ensuring computer security. One industry group estimates that the federal government would need to spend \$2.5 billion to protect its most important computer systems, though actual costs could differ significantly.[36] This approach is consistent with a tiered approach to improving the nation's defenses. Government systems are often very important, either for ensuring national security or for administering programs like Social Security, so they should be well protected—for their own sake and to establish general standards that the private sector might then emulate.

The government also needs to employ a sufficient number of skilled information technology (IT) professionals to protect its systems. Corresponding salaries, work environment, and expectations on length of service must better reflect the private IT labor market. The government needs to be able to attract energetic, up-to-date computer experts, often just for short-term service, rather than rely on the traditional career government bureaucrat who may be less likely to keep up with trends in computing and cybersecurity. The government could offer loan forgiveness and other incentives to recent college graduates with computer expertise to encourage them to join the Civil Service. It could also increase the attractiveness of the so-called senior level (SL) and scientific or professional (ST) positions within the Civil Service.[37] And, adapting a proposal of Richard Betts for intelligence specialists, it could create a type of reserve system for IT security specialists ("weekend cyberwarriors") to be called on when needed.[38]

It is also important that the government ensure sufficient funding for research and development on products such as cybersecurity software. Taking a longer-term view, it is also appropriate for the government to adopt measures to increase domestic expertise in information technology and computer security. It could provide college scholarships for students with majors in cybersecurity, for example.

Several policy measures are warranted to improve cybersecurity at private firms. The government should carefully consider regulating firms that perform critical societal functions—for example, by requiring them to undertake regular "red-team" exercises to assess their vulnerabilities, report the results, and demonstrate that they have made the required repairs when appropriate. It could also require that security features be activated before computers are delivered to customers. And it could push private firms to begin to use physical tokens, possibly including biometric identification, rather than simple passwords to ensure that only authorized users have access to certain machines and accounts.[39]

In addition, as the National Research Council has noted, the government should use market forces to enhance security. It could do so by increasing the legal liability of private firms that fail to exercise due diligence for losses suffered in a cyberattack by their customers or society as a whole. Insurance policies covering companies for various kinds of disruption to service could also be required to develop graduated rate structures that would be influenced by a company's past performance and its preparations to prevent cyberattack.[40]

Military information systems are even harder to address through arms control or any other cooperative mechanisms. This is mitigated by the fact that, although U.S. military networks have already been attacked, most of those that have been attacked were not critical for military operations. For attacks that could inflict harm, major security steps are essential, going beyond frequent password changes and red-team exercises to the creation of redundant networks, isolated networks that are not connected to the Internet, or networks that have more key information hardwired into them to allow rapid network recovery after rebooting "purges."[41]

Expounding on those steps would take a book unto itself, and none of those steps would be arms control. Indeed, cybersecurity in general is not a realm where arms control has anything major to offer. Some coordination of international efforts against hackers and spammers would be wise. But a combination of domestic law enforcement, possible punishment of countries tolerating illicit and destructive computer activity in their territory, and robust defensive measures is what is truly needed.

Conclusion

The challenges posed by the new technologies considered in this chapter—biotechnology, nanotechnology, and information technology—are difficult to address through arms control. Arms control may have a role, but more often when it is envisioned as coordinated domestic action by individual countries rather than as a system of treaty regimes. Such domestic action should feature tough security standards for the people and facilities involved in research on advanced biological agents, for example. It should impose criminal penalties on those violating standards. And it should be sure not to interfere with vigorous research on defenses against advanced pathogens.

That said, it is still important to develop an acceptable regimen for promoting transparency and monitoring in the biological sciences. Admittedly, traditional on-site arms control inspections can easily fail, particularly given the small size of facilities needed to perform advanced research and the ease with which they can be hidden in closed societies. Moreover, the international community absolutely must avoid creating a biological monitoring regime that repeats the key mistake of the Nuclear Non-Proliferation Treaty: making it politically easier for even closed societies with extremist governments to gain access to dangerous technologies by requiring them simply to accept relatively unobtrusive and ineffective inspections. In particular, any verification protocol of the Biological Weapons Convention should clarify that it does not and will not encourage biological trade with such countries.

But a biological oversight system involving at least some on-site inspections can make it easier, when combined with information from intelligence agents, whistleblowers, and the like, to detect illicit activity. Countries trying to hide weapons programs tend not to volunteer the locations of those programs, meaning that verification databases will not include them—so if research activity at such sites is in some way detected later, there will be a stronger basis for suspecting illicit activity. That may not prevent such activity directly, but it will give the international community a stronger position from which to consider various kinds of coercive or punitive measures. Arms control thus has a key role to play, even if, again, its purpose is as much to help provide early warning of violations and to complement a system of stronger defenses as it is to prevent proliferation.

CHAPTER 5

Compelling Compliance

A successful arms control regime must also have the means to enforce its standards. Indeed, enforcement has always been the Achilles' heel of arms control. To a large extent, that was unavoidable: historically, most arms control agreements were between the United States and the Soviet Union, against either of which coercive action, and military action in particular, was unthinkable. Moreover, strict enforcement of nonproliferation rules was undervalued by many countries. For example, that India and Pakistan had acquired nuclear weapons capabilities was considered to be, while troublesome, primarily a regional problem unworthy of costly opposition. Both of these views have changed dramatically in recent years. Those who have most egregiously violated nonproliferation standards—Iran and North Korea, to take the most prominent current examples—are not superpowers, but regional rogues, like Iraq was, that can be effectively opposed. Few call for stern measures against India and Pakistan, but the proliferation precedent they helped set is now widely seen as one to counter strenuously elsewhere. And since September 11, 2001, the United States has understood all too well that enforcement is not a luxury: nuclear or advanced biological weapons in hostile or even *indifferent* hands anywhere are a danger at home.

The standards of acceptable behavior outlined in chapters 3 and 4 should underpin efforts aimed at more effective enforcement. As has been seen with North Korea and is understood with Iran, forcibly stopping a state that is on the brink of acquiring nuclear or advanced biological weapons is often not possible; effective action must be taken earlier. The international community must take enforcement action when states violate certain strict standards, for example, by

—rejecting high transparency standards for nuclear and biological programs

—building new plutonium reprocessing facilities

—producing highly enriched uranium

—refusing to place new uranium enrichment facilities under multinational control

—failing to secure nuclear weapons and materials and biological technology at home

—acquiring nuclear or advanced biological weapons.

When any one of these lines is crossed, coercive measures designed to reverse the proliferation activity and to deter further violations should be strongly considered, even if diplomatic options continue to be explored. Whether a state has technically withdrawn from the Nuclear Non-Proliferation Treaty or the Biological Weapons Convention should be immaterial, and the United States and its allies should lead an effort to obtain UN Security Council endorsement of this stance. The specific tools to be applied must be sensitive to the specific case, as we discuss below. But the list of unacceptable activities should be simple, clear, and universally binding in order to maximize its legitimacy, international support, and ability to deter.

With a new arms control framework as a backdrop, how should decisionmakers determine what measures are warranted? In part, the response will depend on the nature of the state taking unacceptable action. The United States has its own short list of nemeses, with North Korea and Iran now the featured cases. On a slightly lower tier, others consistently named by the United States include Syria, Cuba, and Sudan. A final category of states that concern Washington includes those that it would not officially identify as such, even though many Americans realize that they pose challenges to Western security interests. These are neither true allies nor true adversaries; they may help the United States in some ways while either condoning or failing to prevent extremely dangerous activities of some private citizens and organizations, and possibly parts of their governments, on their soil. This category includes, for example, Belarus, Saudi Arabia, Egypt, Yemen, and Pakistan, as well as others. Due to the mixed cooperative-adversarial relationship the United States has with these states, they are unlikely to become the target of strong coercive measures. But any security guarantees or other assistance that the United States offered to such countries would have to be contingent on their efforts to reform, to combat proliferation, and to avoid the aggressive use of force against other states. Moreover, they should often continue to be targets of milder coercive measures, such as export controls.

The American lists are not without merit, but they are somewhat arbitrary from an international perspective. It is important to establish more consistent criteria that the international community can use as a basis for applying discriminatory and coercive measures against states of interest.[1] In the case of humanitarian intervention, the character of the offending state has been a prime criterion for military intervention, suggesting that such an arrangement might work here too.[2] We propose that, in addition to the standards outlined above, the criteria listed below be applied in assessing whether coercive action is warranted. These "regime-related warning flags" are based on evolving accepted practice and practical foreign policy considerations; in one form or another, they have been advocated both by recent American administrations and international relations scholars.[3] When a state has violated nonproliferation standards and a combination of several of the following regime-related warning flags is present, the case for action is strongest:[4]

—undemocratic or illiberal government

—brutal human rights practices

—recent history of aggressive international behavior, especially armed attack on other countries or an ongoing threat to conduct such attacks

—support for terrorism, especially for groups inclined to cause mass casualties.

Each of these warning flags is consistent with the logic of the basic arms control framework proposed in chapter 1. That framework focuses on controlling the technologies and actors most likely to cause mass casualties, on ensuring transparency and early warning, on possible coercive action, and on providing security incentives for nonproliferating states. From this perspective, undemocratic or illiberal governments pose a transparency and early warning problem. For example, while lengthy public debate normally would probably precede a democratic state's decision to move closer to acquiring nuclear weapons, such a shift in an illiberal state could come suddenly, leaving little time for diplomacy or enforcement action. A history of brutal domestic human rights practices disposes a state to be more willing to kill enemy civilians, including massive numbers of them if nuclear or advanced biological weapons are available. A recent history of aggressive international behavior indicates a similar danger; moreover, a state armed with nuclear or advanced biological weapons, and with a tendency toward aggression, will provoke its neighbors to seek similar arms. Finally, support for terrorist groups makes the danger of nuclear weapons transfer—which the framework outlined above seeks to prevent—more likely.

States judged to be a danger because of both proliferation activity and regime-related warning flags would thus be the most likely targets for coercive enforcement. But even such a set of criteria is only a starting point. For example, how does one address a country that meets some but not all of the criteria? Or what if a country is gradually moving toward more participatory government and better human rights practices even as it continues to fall short of Western norms? And when should coercive actions extend to the ultimate measure—forcible overthrow of a regime? To illustrate how the criteria can be applied, we analyze a number of cases, both past and present, including several of acute concern today. The particular approaches outlined below do not follow automatically and unambiguously from our arms control framework—other reasonable approaches are possible—but they illustrate one way that enforcement might be done within the framework.

Preemption and Prevention

Before analyzing individual cases, it is instructive to contrast the basic approach outlined above with the Bush administration's preemption doctrine as codified in the 2002 National Security Strategy (NSS), which has been promoted as the key to enforcing nonproliferation standards. While there is much that is logical in the thinking behind that strategy, it is at best an incomplete guide for dealing with proliferation crises, and in some important ways it is counterproductive.

Preemption defined as the anticipatory use of force in the face of an imminent attack has long been accepted as legitimate and appropriate under international law and by American presidents. In the 2002 NSS, however, the Bush administration broadened the meaning to encompass preventive war as well, in which force may be used even without evidence of an imminent attack to ensure that a serious threat to the United States does not "gather" or grow over time. The so-called preemption doctrine is thus something of a misnomer, because its sweep is even broader than that term suggests. The strategy also elevated the importance and visibility of preventive war as a tool of U.S. foreign policy.

The doctrine of preemption was not needed for the largely successful military campaign in Afghanistan starting in 2001, since that operation was easily justified as self-defense under Article 51 of the United Nations charter, even if it was also simple retaliation. Nor, despite its invocation, was it needed to make the case for the U.S.-led overthrow of Saddam Hussein, since Hussein was in violation of more than a dozen U.N. Security Council resolutions, making it legally justifiable for the international community to end the 1991 cease-fire. (Whether it was wise to terminate that cease-fire and invade Iraq is another matter, which we discuss below.)

Current American preemption doctrine does not claim to apply to all countries, only terrorist organizations and so-called rogue states. The Bush administration has argued that the continued spread of WMD technology to states with a history of aggression presents a "compelling . . . case for taking anticipatory action to defend ourselves, even if uncertainty remains as to the time and place of the enemy's attack."[5] As Secretary of State Colin Powell explained the rationale in early 2004, the preemption doctrine was designed to explain to the American people that its government possessed the common sense needed to decide how to protect the country in a time of terror. It was further intended to put U.S. enemies on notice that if their behavior did not radically and quickly change, "they were in big trouble."[6] Powell also asserted that observers had overestimated the centrality of preemption in administration policy. That point seems fair if one reads the entire National Security Strategy cover to cover, given the document's emphasis on other tools of foreign policy, such as deterrence. But the point seems forced if one recognizes that it was the Bush administration itself that chose to emphasize its new focus on preemption.

Elevating preemption to a matter of doctrine and including the preventive option within the doctrine can have serious negative consequences, whether it is applied broadly or for more narrow arms control purposes. It reinforces the image of the United States as too quick to use military force and to do so outside the bounds of international law and legitimacy, for its own purposes based on its own judgment. This can make it more difficult for the United States to gain international support for its use of force, complicating its pursuit of a necessarily muscular approach to arms control; it can also provoke some adversaries to seek the very weapons the United States wishes to deny them. But critics of the

Bush administration's preemption doctrine should not go so far as to deny the importance of a stern and credible policy toward proliferation of weapons of mass destruction. Such a policy can help deter states from pursuing weapons of mass destruction; for example, it was probably a factor in Libyan leader Moammar Qaddafi's decision in late 2003 to give up his country's weapons of mass destruction. It would be a mistake to give the preemption doctrine full credit for this development, which followed a number of other positive steps by Libya in recent years that predated it. But it would also be unconvincing to deny that the doctrine, and the overthrow of Saddam Hussein, had at least some role.

Preemption doctrine and the U.S. list of rogue states are not up to the task of guiding enforcement of nonproliferation standards. An approach that includes more options and can elicit broader international support would be more effective. But is such an approach possible and practical? Its ultimate test would be the hard cases, several of which are considered below.

Case Studies

A general arms control approach does not suffice for dealing individually with what have been the tough cases—Iraq, North Korea, Iran, Syria, India, and Pakistan. That will also be true for difficult proliferation problems in the future. Other foreign policy considerations and practical details concerning timing and context, which are always important in real-world policymaking, are critical. In addition, judgment will always be required; there are no mechanical rules that can be developed and then automatically applied to determine when and how to use coercion against dangerous countries. Instead, a new arms control framework must establish the proper general boundaries of plausible policy options as well as a sense of which types of countries and problems merit special attention.

Some broad observations about the six specific countries mentioned above can be made immediately. First, Iraq and North Korea—each led by a brutal dictatorial regime with a history of blatant aggression and horrible human rights practices and each having been uncooperative over a decade of concerted arms control efforts—required stern measures when their proliferation-related behavior became extreme. Syria, by contrast, is a somewhat less egregiously oppressive regime with a far less threatening program of weapons of mass destruction. In this context, its chemical and biological programs, while highly undesirable, do not require the type of extreme coercive measures or urgent diplomatic attention that Iraq and North Korea have demanded in recent times. Iran is somewhere in between. Especially if its government continues to reinforce its autocratic hold on power at home while sustaining or stepping up terrorist activities as it pursues a nuclear program, urgent attention will increasingly be required. That may not translate into military force. But conducting business as usual with Tehran should not be an option if its behavior does not improve on any of the fronts mentioned. India and especially Pakistan have done the cause of international nonproliferation no favors through their recent behavior. But it is unrealistic to try to convince Islamabad or New Delhi to reverse its nuclear program, and their general foreign policy behavior does not warrant a strong coercive response from the international community. That said, some means of restraining their future nuclear-related activities is badly needed to check the damage caused by their proliferant behavior. Finally, though most of these cases focus on nuclear weapons, that is not because advanced biological weapons are less worrying but simply reflects the decisions and capabilities of today's most problematic countries. The lessons learned from these nuclear cases may well apply to advanced biological threats in the future. Each case is discussed in more detail below.

Iraq

Within the broad context of arms control, one can debate the need for the war to overthrow Saddam Hussein, and it is certainly far from clear that the U.S.-led military operation has improved Western security. That said, strong proponents of arms control should have at least some sympathy for the Bush administration's approach to dealing with Saddam Hussein in the months leading up to war in March 2003. Much of what Bush did was consistent with—even exemplary of—the argument in this book. The Bush administration and its partners focused on the most dangerous technologies in the hands of a leader who was one of the world's most difficult to control. They used a robust monitoring system (developed and maintained by their predecessors and the United Nations) to gain early warning of possible illicit weapons programs. They treated the Iraqi lack of transparency as a grave arms control offense—as they were right to do, whether Iraq had in fact eliminated its weapons stockpiles or not, because the world community had no reason to believe Saddam's claims of disarmament without proof. They considered Iraq's violation of extremely serious arms control commitments to establish a predicate for military enforcement. Their greatest failing, in terms of arms control, was their inability to garner broad international support for the eventual war and their tendency to conflate the most dangerous technologies, especially nuclear weapons, with other less dangerous weapons of mass destruction.

Many would argue that the Bush administration did not use Iraqi noncompliance as an honest predicate for war but as an excuse for waging a war it wanted for other reasons. Others assert that even if Iraq was admittedly in serious noncompliance with its obligations to allow the international community to verify its disarmament, a policy of containment was preferable under the circumstances. Such a debate is inevitable and indeed critical when a broad conceptual construct is applied to specific decisions about waging war. The Bush administration ought not to be excused for its unilateralist decision to go to war, a major error that largely undid all the hard work that the United States had done until then in forging a broad coalition dedicated to the legal and reasonable cause of forcing Iraq to honor its disarmament obligations. Nonetheless, the arms control framework developed here could have guided the Bush administration's actions and counseled it to do many of the same things.

The Bush administration's policies in forging UN Security Council Resolution 1441 in the fall of 2002 were strongly consistent with the new approach to arms control offered here. First, the administration recognized that it confronted a brutal dictator with a history of internal and external aggression who was also refusing to comply with his country's international obligations not to pursue weapons of mass destruction and to disarm transparently. Strengthening the case further, Saddam had actually used weapons of mass destruction in the past, including against defenseless civilians. His track record satisfied most of the criteria we identify for paying special attention to a problem case—proliferant behavior, likelihood of aggressive intent, nondemocratic and illiberal governance, egregious human rights violations, and flouting of international norms against the use of weapons of mass destruction. The resolution's demands that Saddam go beyond the inspection practices of the 1990s to allow inspectors to interview weapons scientists and that he prove his compliance rather than simply allow inspectors to roam his country corrected some of the problems of the previous inspections experience in Iraq; those demands also reflected a logic similar to that of several of the recommendations made in this book. The resolution also conveyed a sense of urgency that was necessary if the world's attention was not to be gradually distracted from Iraq.

Iraq's subsequent weapons declaration on December 7, 2002, did not meet the demands of Resolution 1441. Even if the Iraqi dictator no longer possessed weapons of mass destruction at that point, he was under obligation to prove that fact by explaining what he had done with all the materials he had previously imported that had no plausible purpose other than to produce chemical or biological arms—a demand for transparency that we have argued is central to the future of arms control. He did not do so. He was also required to produce weapons scientists with knowledge of the history of his weapons programs, something our arms control framework would institutionalize, but few such individuals ever came forward. The resulting situation was intolerable.

Admittedly, the strategic imperative of completely disarming Saddam through immediate resort to military force could be debated, and the arms control framework presented here leaves space for that debate. The inspections and disarmament actions conducted through 1998 and the sanctions that continued thereafter had limited his capacity to develop weapons of mass destruction and in particular the most dangerous among them, nuclear and advanced biological weapons. There was also a reasonable case that Saddam might be contained, at least for a time, based on the previous dozen years of relatively restrained behavior on his part.

In addition, the Bush administration badly mishandled how it chose to go to war. Without formally announcing that Saddam's December 7 weapons declaration provided the legal basis for war—since Resolution 1441 did not state that a faulty declaration could itself justify the use of military force—the administration began to deploy large military forces to the Persian Gulf region. In fact, Iraq did not significantly interfere with inspectors or otherwise compound its existing infractions, forcing the Bush administration to make a decision about going to war based on evidence that most viewed as incomplete—and that the administration itself had not immediately seized on as sufficient justification for war. Since the size of the U.S. military buildup to the region was implausibly large for the purpose of compelling compliance alone, the decision to go to war was in effect already made. That meant that the United States had "ambushed" France and other countries skeptical of the case for the imminent overthrow of Saddam just as much as France then "ambushed" the Bush administration by declaring in January that there was no case for war.

Much can be debated, and much was surely done badly by the United States and its coalition. But the basic decision to confront Saddam with the possibility of coercive action and to demand maximum transparency on his part was appropriate given the arms control and other security issues at stake.

North Korea

The ongoing North Korean nuclear crisis poses another major test for arms control. As with Iraq, the situation crosses our framework's threshold for demanding a robust response from the international community. The most dangerous technologies known to mankind are involved, and they are in the hands of a problem regime. A fairly vigorous arms control system has been established to provide early warning of dangerous behavior, and it has done that. Arms control as a purely diplomatic exercise has already been proven to fail in dealing with Pyongyang; therefore it has a reasonable chance of success only when linked to potentially more coercive action on the part of the international community.

When it began to develop a uranium enrichment program, North Korea (DPRK) violated not only the 1994 Agreed Framework with the United States, under which it pledged not to develop or possess nuclear weapons, but also the Nuclear Non-Proliferation Treaty and the 1991 North-South denuclearization pact with Seoul. It then claimed to withdraw from the NPT, but only after violating it—an action of questionable legality and strategically unacceptable consequences. It also expelled IAEA inspectors, further contravening its NPT obligations and eliminating necessary transparency.[7]

The framework offered here thus counsels the United States and the international community to make it a top security priority not to allow North Korea to develop a nuclear arsenal and, ideally, to ultimately roll back the small nuclear capability North Korea may already have.[8] There are several reasons why such an arsenal would pose a grave risk, each of which reflects more generic concerns described earlier. First, if it develops substantial amounts of fissile material, North Korea might sell some to terrorists or to other states; if North Korea is desperate enough, such an action might hold appeal even if the international community had a good chance of uncovering evidence of the transaction. Second, if North Korea someday collapses, its nuclear materials could fall into the hands of those who would sell them to the highest bidder. Third, U.S.-South Korea deterrence could be weakened if North Korea thought it had a nuclear trump card. Should war then result, the more bombs North Korea possessed, the greater its odds of successfully delivering a nuclear warhead against Seoul or another population center (even in the United States, probably by means other than missile attack). Finally, North Korea's possession of nuclear weapons could start a nuclear domino effect in Northeast Asia, possibly provoking Japan, South Korea, and Taiwan to develop nuclear weapons programs, which would in turn weaken global nonproliferation efforts and perhaps destabilize East Asia.

Applying the arms control logic developed above to North Korea suggests another ultimatum strategy for dealing with the problem. Since North Korea has generally shown restraint toward South Korea (the ROK) and the United States for well over a decade and since no war has been fought against those countries under Kim Jong Il, an engagement policy is worth trying provided that it is tough-minded. The United States and its regional partners, South Korea, Japan, China, and Russia, should offer Pyongyang a set of inducements as well as a clear threat that the nuclear status quo, or worse, cannot and will not be accepted, as elaborated below. In doing so they should be careful not to set a precedent for rewarding illicit behavior by granting North Korea significant benefits simply for undoing a nuclear program that it should not have had in the first place. (One approach might demand structural economic reform, other arms control steps, and human rights improvements in North Korea as further conditions for substantial aid.)

It would be ideal to use a UN Security Council resolution, leveraging arms control standards, to codify these demands and give greater legitimacy to any use of sanctions or even military force that might ultimately be contemplated. The agreement of the regional parties is probably more crucial than that of the Security Council, since they are the countries that would be most affected by any war—though again, arms control standards should be used to help create consensus. But there is little reason to think that the Security Council would fail to endorse a policy that South Korea, Japan, China, Russia, and the United States all supported. Active UN support would also help give credibility to the argument that the international community should adopt the new approach to arms control advocated here.

Given North Korea's worries about the Bush administration's doctrine of preemption and its initiation of military action against Iraq in 2003, it might not be feasible to convince the DPRK to give up all of its nuclear capabilities immediately.[9] It might take several years to reach that final goal, perhaps even until the end of the decade. But the United States could accept most deals that immediately and verifiably froze the DPRK's nuclear activities and quickly began to get plutonium out of North Korea.

Should negotiations fail, the option of coercive action should be retained. The notion of a last-resort, "surgical" military strike against the plutonium fuel rods at Yongbyon no longer makes sense, since North Korea appears to have removed the plutonium that was there. But economic coercion should still be feasible, although admittedly it would have less likelihood of immediate success. And war to cause regime change could still be kept as a last resort, despite its horrible consequences, particularly if North Korea's behavior became even more unpredictable or dangerous.[10]

Iran

Iran presents a difficult test for the future of arms control. Evaluated according to our criteria, the problem is of the utmost seriousness: extremely dangerous technologies are involved, a state with strong links to terrorism is pursuing them, attempts to achieve greater arms control transparency are being made but are frequently stymied, and the case for coercive measures is thus rather strong. Unlike North Korea, though, Iran has not already progressed to the point of having nuclear weapons. And unlike with Iraq, where nonmilitary efforts at resolution failed for more than a decade, concerted diplomatic efforts with Iran have just begun. Finally, despite discouraging recent trends in Iran's politics, the country is not nearly so dictatorial as Iraq under Saddam or North Korea under Kim. Internal political reform may help the nonproliferation cause—and the reform process may be affected by how the outside world pressures Tehran. (This is not because a more liberal government would necessarily want nuclear weapons less, but because such a government could be more sensitive to the associated penalties.) Under these circumstances, the new approach to arms control would lead to a focus on pressing for greater transparency and stricter controls on Iranian activities. At the same time, it would suggest using the time available to probe Iran's amenity to diplomacy, while preserving the possibility of using arms control as a predicate for coercion.

There is no doubt that Iran has already transgressed many nonproliferation commitments. By lying to IAEA inspectors and conducting secret uranium enrichment and plutonium reprocessing experiments over eighteen years, Iran has explicitly violated its NPT obligations, which require transparency and monitoring for any such efforts even when not related to weapons development. Compounding those specific violations, Iran has consistently supported international terrorism, including by sponsoring

Hezbollah and reportedly harboring al Qaeda operatives, and it has a poor human rights record, though its transgressions are not of the same scale as North Korea's or Iraq's under Saddam Hussein.

By most measures, Iran is currently the world's number-one state sponsor of terrorism, given its active support for Hezbollah in particular. Iran may be less likely than North Korea to sell fissile materials to terrorists to earn money, but given its long-standing relationship with Hezbollah, it would be more likely to use terrorists to execute state policy. If it had a nuclear deterrent, it might not fear American (or Israeli) retribution as acutely and might be even less constrained about unleashing Hezbollah or other terrorist groups. Iran's acquisition of nuclear arms could directly spur regional competitors—in particular, Egypt, Saudi Arabia, and Syria, possibly other countries—to acquire their own. And while the failure to stop North Korea from acquiring nuclear arms can be blamed in part on past policy errors, if Iran were to acquire an atomic bomb it would suggest that the United States and the international community—even with their new focus on preventing proliferation and even with relatively early warning of proliferation activity—are effectively powerless to stop the spread of nuclear weapons. It would thus be an invitation to any would-be proliferators.

To achieve confidence that Iran will not acquire nuclear weapons, the specific goals in this situation should be to get Iran to completely accept the Additional Protocol of the NPT—a transparency requirement our arms control framework advocates for all nuclear programs—for the nuclear technology it now possesses or seeks to obtain (preventing its acquisition of reactors does not appear to be feasible by anything short of military means). Iran must also be required to shut down its uranium enrichment program, a penalty that our framework advocates for states that breach their nonproliferation obligation. Without the Additional Protocol, the world would have little chance of detecting any hidden second track of Iran's nuclear program. And if the uranium enrichment program remains in Iran's control, the world would have little warning to enable it to oppose an Iranian breakout leading to the production of highly enriched uranium. Ideally, a successful strategy would also eliminate Iran's heavy-water reactor program, which can provide a cover for developing reprocessing technology.

The United States and its allies must be careful not to offer too much in exchange simply for curbs on the Iranian nuclear program, since they should not bribe countries to keep their existing nonproliferation obligations and since they must retain leverage to deal with the Iranian terrorism problem. But the EU and the United States should offer cooperation on non-nuclear energy pursuits, and the United States should be prepared to gradually ease trade restrictions in the event of commensurate Iranian progress in restraining its support for terrorism.

If Iran is unwilling to make the necessary concessions and conform to the new arms control standards, the United States and its allies will need to adopt a more coercive strategy. Such a strategy would start with Europe, Japan, and ideally Russia making future improvements in relations with Iran contingent on Iran's acceptance of the nonproliferation demands. They would also have to halt sales of uranium and other nuclear-related technologies to Iran. These steps should be taken even as attempts are made to negotiate a solution using economic and diplomatic incentives. If such attempts at engagement have clearly failed, the United States should attempt to obtain economic sanctions against Iran through the UN Security Council if possible and with a smaller coalition if necessary, in either case using Iran's arms control violations as the explicit predicate for action. Proliferation Security Initiative participants also should devote resources to interdicting Iran-bound illicit technology shipments.

The United States and its allies should also warn Tehran of actions that they might take should it further violate its NPT obligations and proceed toward achieving nuclear weapons capability. These measures should be considered particularly seriously should Iran sustain or accelerate its support for terrorism.

First, if Iran ejects IAEA inspectors, the United States and its allies should quickly seek a Security Council resolution requiring the IAEA to remove all safeguarded uranium and plutonium from Iran. Russia could execute the actual removal if Tehran did not forcibly resist the action. The resolution should also authorize the IAEA to disable whatever enrichment and fuel conversion plants Iran is pursuing. If such a resolution is not forthcoming or if Iran resists its implementation, the United States and its allies could destroy the Natanz enrichment plant and the Isfahan fuel-processing plant. If none of these steps is taken, Iran's nuclear status will be ambiguous at best—an intolerable situation according to the broad principles we advocate for future arms control. In the unlikely event that the United States can develop an option to deprive Iran of access to the Bushehr reactor—for example, by repeatedly bombing the vicinity with delayed-fuse munitions—it should consider doing so. Also, if Iran attempts to withdraw fuel from its Bushehr reactor before it is completely irradiated—that is, when it is optimized for weapons use—the United States and its allies could attack any identifiable plutonium processing facilities to which the fuel might be moved. Such measures may not prove advisable, depending on specific circumstances—but in some cases they will be the preferred course of action.

Syria

Syria is alleged to be pursuing nuclear, chemical, and biological weapons programs, along with ballistic missiles. It is also a state sponsor of terrorism. But while worthy of careful attention, its behavior should not, according to our criteria, rise yet to the level of concern recently accorded to Iraq, North Korea, and Iran. Most important, Syria's well-developed WMD programs focus primarily on chemical weapons, not nuclear or advanced biological arms. In addition, its support for terrorism, while serious, does not pose the same magnitude of threat to Western security as has Iran's for Hezbollah, and its territorial ambitions appear to be more modest than those of Iraq under Saddam Hussein or of North Korea.

According to the Central Intelligence Agency, "Russia and Syria have approved a draft cooperative program on cooperation on civil nuclear power. In principle, broader access to Russian expertise provides opportunities for Syria to expand its indigenous capabilities, should it decide to pursue nuclear weapons."[11] There is also some suspicion that Syria was a client of Pakistani scientist A. Q. Khan's nuclear trading network.[12] There is little direct evidence, however, of significant advances in Syria's nuclear program. According to Bush administration under secretary of state John Bolton, the United States "continue[s] to watch for any sign of nuclear weapons activity or foreign assistance that could facilitate a Syrian nuclear weapons capability."[13]

Further, there is little definitive evidence of a sophisticated Syrian biological weapons program, an issue that we will discuss in more depth in the next chapter. According to a recent CIA report, "It is highly probable that Syria also is continuing to develop an offensive BW capability." Little further evidence has been presented. According to Bolton, "we believe Syria would need foreign assistance to launch a large-scale biological weapons program right now."[14]

In light of this analysis, no drastic steps are warranted with regard to Syria's WMD programs. The United States should focus on preventing advanced biological technology exports—through the Australia Group, an export control coalition discussed further in the next chapter, and, if possible, the Proliferation Security Initiative. To improve transparency and to probe Syria's intent, it should also pursue Syria's ratification of the Additional Protocol to the NPT. The United States should also press for Syrian ratification of the Biological Weapons Convention (BWC), including, if it can be acceptably negotiated, a new verification protocol to the BWC.

None of this should be read as excluding the possibility of more forceful action against Syria for other offenses, such as on the terrorism front. Rather, it is simply to say that the Syrian WMD problem is nowhere near a critical state.

Pakistan

Pakistan is a most worrisome case: it has nuclear weapons, little transparency, and a brittle government that might someday be replaced by a much more extreme regime with sympathies toward terrorist groups. The current regime would hardly countenance giving up its nuclear programs, and as argued earlier, rolling back India's and Pakistan's programs should not be an active goal of arms control policy. Instead, the current focus of policy should be on finding a nonproliferation "halfway house" for Pakistan and India that encourages responsible stewardship of nuclear weapons and related technologies.[15] That would also help address the pressing challenge of proliferation of nuclear weapons to new, dangerous actors. The primary aim on the Pakistani side should be to clamp down on nuclear-related exports by Pakistan and to ensure the security of its arsenal while seeking to cap the quantitative and qualitative development of the arsenal (and to prevent future nuclear testing).

Pakistan presents several major challenges to any American strategy designed to control dangerous technologies in general and nuclear weapons in particular. It has enough extremist elements within its political system to demand constant vigilance and considerable further attention to its arsenal. Pakistan's apparent willingness to export sensitive nuclear technology to North Korea and to Iran (or at least to turn a blind eye to such exports) has been a major blow to cooperative export control regimes as well. Its acquisition of nuclear weapons outside the Nuclear Non-Proliferation Treaty has undeniably weakened the norm against nuclear proliferation. And some suspect that Pakistan would be willing to transfer whole nuclear weapons to other states; Saudi Arabia is frequently mentioned in this respect.

However, several mitigating circumstances have pushed the United States toward a decidedly less confrontational policy toward Pakistan than this indictment might suggest. First, in the immediate aftermath of the September 11 terrorist attacks, the United States urgently needed Pakistani overflight and basing rights and assistance in conducting its war against al Qaeda and the Taliban. This led the United States to lift sanctions on Pakistan related to its nuclear violations. While understandable at the time, this approach should not constitute the entirity of American proliferation policy toward Islamabad.

The United States and allies should use the promise of further economic aid and trade concessions to improve Pakistan's nuclear export controls; at the same time, the United States might provide Pakistan technical assistance in implementing those controls. There is little unclassified knowledge as to the extent of official authorization for Pakistan's past proliferation-related activities, but it is reasonable to assume that at least some may have been unauthorized. The United States should consider discussing methods for enhancing and implementing export controls. It should be very careful, however, not to transfer information that Pakistan or others might use to evade U.S. export controls, as discussed earlier.

It would also be beneficial to bring Pakistan formally into the international non-proliferation regime, in order to give it a political stake in the regime's success. The best way to begin this process would be for Pakistan (and India) to sign and ratify the Comprehensive Test Ban Treaty. In addition to formally involving Pakistan, that would help prevent Pakistan from setting a bad example by further testing nuclear weapons. It will be very difficult politically, though, to achieve such an agreement so long as the United States does not ratify the treaty, as it eventually should. Indian ratification will be essential too. In the interim, the United States should continue to make clear to Pakistan that any resumption of nuclear testing would result in the degradation of the bilateral relationship between the two nations.

In parallel, the United States should try to convince Pakistan to terminate the production of all fissile material for nuclear weapons, as all the major nuclear powers have, as part of the effort to phase out production of weapons-usable material worldwide described earlier. Such specific, realistic, limited requests could succeed—especially if accompanied by corresponding American and Indian actions.

India

India's regime is more stable than Pakistan's and less inclined to support or condone terrorist groups or rogue states. But it is still a concern given its recent record of nuclear testing and its status outside the NPT. A new approach to dealing with India is needed, given the fact that it is extremely unlikely to denuclearize. International engagement with India in the nuclear sphere should focus on three fronts discussed in general earlier in this book: improving export controls; solidifying the global nonproliferation regime through means such as a test ban treaty and a ban on production of fissile materials; and fostering a stable strategic balance with Pakistan (and with China) at the lowest possible level of forces. As with Pakistan, shaping India's nuclear forces would be a lower priority than preventing further proliferation, given the practicalities and realities of the situation. (Some sharing of safety technologies would, as argued earlier, be appropriate.)

Unlike Pakistan, India has demonstrated a real commitment to imposing nuclear export controls. Thus the United States should focus on ensuring that India has the appropriate legal and institutional arrangements to effectively implement its export control goals. In addition, the United States should encourage India to formally declare its intent to comply with the Nuclear Suppliers Group guidelines restricting sensitive nuclear exports. Such a declaration would improve international leverage in pressuring Pakistan to adopt similar standards.[16]

CHAPTER 6

Conventional Arms Control and Regional Conflict

Civil conflicts continue to kill hundreds of thousands of people a year worldwide, and a regional war could put the lives of millions at risk. Any serious attempt at creating a comprehensive arms control strategy must explore whether arms control can make a difference in this terrible reality. Even if it cannot in the end do much, it may contribute somewhat to lessening the risk of armed confrontation—and even modest progress could save many lives. In this way, the new arms control strategy would directly address what are for many non-Western countries their chief security worries. It would also help stabilize conflict zones where terrorists can find safe haven or illegally harvest natural resources to put to illicit ends—or purchase weapons like surface-to-air missiles, which are a particular worry in fighting terrorism.

Although efforts to constrain the weapons inventories of most major powers are no longer a top priority, arms control may still have a role in regulating the military arms balance in certain regions. Individual opportunities—such as in Korea, depending on the course of future negotiations—should not be ignored simply because they may be relatively few in number. A new arms control paradigm should not discard the old in its entirety; there are elements of the bilateral cold war arms control strategy that remain instructive today, even if as a broad approach it is no longer a good guide to action in most situations.

Small Arms

Light weapons such as automatic rifles, mortars, and rocket-propelled grenades cause most of the casualties in ongoing world conflicts today. Hundreds of thousands of people lose their lives annually in these conflicts, either in direct combat or from the famine and disease that often ensue—and while the number is not getting rapidly worse, it is not diminishing very quickly either.[1] Efforts by outside powers to address such conflicts are no longer frequently seen in the developing world as quasi-imperialist actions, but as part of an imperative to act shared by all countries.[2] The United States also worries that small weapons could be used in many types of terrorist attacks; shoulder-launched surface-to-air missiles are of particular concern.[3]

Arms control efforts to reduce trade in these weapons cannot prevent most established countries from obtaining them in whatever quantities desired. The technology for manufacturing them is simple and accessible; moreover, more than 100 million automatic weapons—often costing well under $1,000 or even under $100—are estimated to be on the world market.[4] Nor are curbs always desirable, even in conflict-prone regions. Often it is more advantageous to strengthen the more humane and responsible parties to a conflict rather than try to weaken them along with their enemies. But the right kinds of curbs can reduce the access to such arms of undesirable militias and insurgents and of terrorists—or at least drive the price up and the quantity down. Of course bad elements will still get some weapons, but in many conflicts the quality and quantity of what they can lay their hands on matters.

Tackling this issue requires a highly selective approach to arms control. Maintaining realistic expectations of what it can meaningfully accomplish and making use of other foreign policy and law enforcement tools are a necessary part of the mix.

Using formal arms control to limit the flow of light weapons is hard in part because some arms transfers are actually acceptable, even those to resistance groups, which in some cases have a reasonable case for rebelling against their governments. Just as challenging, the sheer number of suppliers together with the small size of the weapons involved makes it hard to monitor small arms shipments. Indeed, estimates of the value of the trade in small arms are highly uncertain—ranging from $3 billion to $10 billion in the legal trade and perhaps another 10 to 20 percent of that amount in illegal transactions—underscoring the difficulty of monitoring or regulating this commerce.[5] Both legal and illegal sales can cause problems: for example, weapons purchased legally in the United States reportedly constitute much of the arms inventory of drug traffickers in Latin America.[6]

Larger weapons at least can be monitored once deployed by military forces, and they also are produced primarily by a small group of major industrial countries. Five countries, the permanent members of the U.N. Security Council, led by the United States, account for more than 80 percent of all conventional arms transfers, most of which (as assessed by the financial value of the transfers) involve heavy weaponry.[7] The other top suppliers are Ukraine, Germany, Italy, Israel, Brazil, and Spain.[8] A UN Register on Conventional Arms was created in 1991 to promote transparency regarding the trade in such large weapons.

But at least ninety-five countries and thousands of factories are involved in producing smaller arms, and no practical way exists to monitor their output or the inventories of recipient countries.[9] It is generally not feasible to monitor disarmament rigorously and completely even when local parties to a conflict have agreed to monitoring and invited peacekeepers to verify the process.[10]

This problem calls for a multifaceted approach. Direct attempts to limit access to the most dangerous kinds of small arms, such as surface-to-air missiles, are one important element. This is largely a job for intelligence and law enforcement, though it may also be possible to persuade most producers of specific types of dangerous weaponry to improve their vigilance in monitoring production facilities and arms sales. Indeed, national legislatures might go further, requiring installation of use-control mechanisms such as time-expiring locks that would render a weapon unusable after a certain period unless sophisticated tools and codes were available to reset the locks.[11] This approach would complicate the efforts of anyone attempting to make illicit use of a weapon.

Conventions on the small arms trade already exist, under the auspices of the European Union, the Organization of American States, and the UN General Assembly. They focus chiefly on stigmatizing illegal sales—in other words, sales not carried out by properly licensed firms and individuals. However, often what is needed is a broader definition of what is illegal in a number of important supplier countries and improved monitoring of sales. Further stigmatization of what is currently illegal is not an adequate policy response.[12]

Existing regulations provide a starting point for further measures, if they can be extended to more countries and in some cases toughened. For example, the NGO-proposed code of conduct for U.S. arms exporters, which emphasizes that potential weapons recipients must have a demonstrated commitment to human rights and democracy and a history of nonaggression toward neighbors, has merit.[13] Though not law, even in the United States, it has gained increasing influence in congressional oversight of the arms trade. Its goals are in some cases too ambitious—sales to Pakistan and Saudi Arabia are the most obvious. Sometimes a balance must be struck between immediate national security imperatives and ideal objectives. This can be acceptable provided that the countries in question are evolving in a generally positive direction, are not acting aggressively toward their neighbors, and are relatively benign in their treatment of their own citizens. Blatant violators of these conditions, however, need to be constrained. The International Committee of the Red Cross has promoted similar concepts more globally.[14]

Useful concepts have also come out of recent efforts of the European Union and the United Nations.[15] The EU effort is similar to the proposed code of conduct for U.S. arms exporters. It relies strictly on national enforcement, but it does put governments in communication with each other and makes their arms sales policies transparent, increasing the chances that if one country denies an export, others will too. The UN Protocol against the Illicit Manufacturing of and Trafficking in Firearms, Their Parts and Components, and Ammunition requires documenting all stages of the arms sales process as well as putting indelible markings on weapons to make them easier to trace.[16] And a 1998 African initiative flatly banned arms trading in West Africa.[17] More countries should also pass laws banning exports to countries or groups that have been prohibited by UN resolution from receiving arms.[18]

These tools are not sufficiently robust to ensure a high level of compliance, but they are, at a minimum, useful law enforcement mechanisms for increasing the chances that illegal or destructive arms sales to especially dangerous groups will be discouraged or stopped. They also improve the odds that in those extreme cases in which the UN Security Council bans sales to an especially vicious group or government, mechanisms will be in place to curtail shipments to that party.

Limiting the Financial Resources of Extremist Groups

Another policy mechanism available to address the problem of civil conflict and small arms trading is to limit the financial resources available to extremist nonstate groups. Less money means less ability to buy arms. This is not arms control per se, since no direct restrictions or surveillance are imposed on the arms trade. But it is tightly linked to the arms trade and can be used to achieve the same ends as more direct approaches.

An important example of such an approach is the Kimberley Process, which helps to ensure that the global diamond trade does not involve "blood diamonds" mined by violent groups, including al Qaeda. Recognizing that most of the international supply of high-quality diamonds already comes from reputable suppliers, the system tracks diamonds from source to store. Most major suppliers and most members of the Organization for Economic Cooperation and Development (OECD) are signatories of this 2002 accord. A total of seventy-six countries were involved as of July 2003, with fifty-four in proper standing and twenty-two still lagging in their implementation of domestic legislation to authorize the new regime. Some argue for international verification of the accord, but this may not be necessary to achieve most of its benefits.[19] Diamonds are placed in tagged containers that are difficult to reproduce, and seals are used to ensure that the containers are not opened in transit. Given the modest quantity of the commerce and the high prices associated with gems, using such security measures does not add much in percentage terms to the price of the commodity.[20]

A related approach could be applied to monitoring trade in lumber. While the value per pound of product is clearly far less than for gems, large individual tropical trees are enormously valuable and modern tracking and identification devices costing only a few dollars are thus easily affordable. A good deal of illegal logging funds conflicts in places such as West Africa. The G-8 governments promoted the idea of such monitoring in Okinawa in 1999. Further steps could include placing penalties on companies caught not abiding by the new regulations.

Together, measures taken to ensure arms sales transparency, establish codes of conduct, pay special attention to particularly dangerous technologies, groups, and governments, and clamp down on the finances of such groups and governments make good sense. But one must be careful not to think that because some arms control measures are good, more would be even better. The sheer number of suppliers, relatively low cost of the technologies involved, and the challenge of verification would likely make any overly ambitious scheme counterproductive. Addressing the problems of failed states and civil conflict will depend even more on other types of policy instruments, such as forceful diplomacy, economic carrots and sticks, and at times forcible humanitarian military intervention.

Land Mines

Land mines have been the subject of rigorous international attention in recent years, and in 1997 the Ottawa Convention was concluded, banning their possession and use. Land mines are a global humanitarian scourge much more than a military problem. They claim thousands of victims a year—mostly civilians in developing countries, where mines often continue to lurk in farmers' fields, villagers' walkways, and children's playgrounds after conflicts are over.[21] That means that de-mining must be a central element of any country's post-conflict plan for stopping the carnage of war and generating economic recovery. Many advocate that formal arms control be used to discourage the further spread and use of these devices.[22]

The Ottawa Convention (The 1997 Convention on the Prohibition of the Use, Stockpiling, Production and Transfer of Anti-Personnel Mines and on Their Destruction) went into force in early 1999. It has loopholes and flaws; it does not cover mixed mines, which contain antipersonnel as well as antivehicle components, if the primary purpose of the mixed mines is to stop vehicles, and it does not cover strictly antivehicle mines either.[23] Nearly 150 countries are now signatories, but the United States is not. The United States continues to abide by the 1996 amended mines protocol of the Convention on Certain Conventional Weapons (CCCW), which among other things requires mines delivered by artillery or aircraft to have self-deactivation mechanisms. In 1998, the Clinton administration went most but not all of the way toward supporting the Ottawa Convention, agreeing to end the use of antipersonnel land mines outside Korea by 2003 and to eliminate them even there by 2006 if suitable alternatives could be found.

The Bush administration rejected the Ottawa accord and decided to support a different approach to land mine control. Other nonsignatories as of this writing include Russia (which, according to some analysts, feels that land mines are necessary to protect its nuclear power plants), China (which cites its long land borders), and South Korea (for reasons similar to those of the United States).[24]

The Ottawa Convention is not inconsistent with American security interests, given the relatively modest role land mines play in legitimate military operations today; for example, having used more than 100,000 land mines in Operation Desert Storm in 1991, coalition forces did not employ them in the overthrow of Saddam Hussein in 2003.[25] But land mines are not an arms control priority rivaling nuclear and biological weapons, or even small arms. So many land mines are available and they are so easy to make that a black market is likely to continue in them regardless of international convention. Still, if that were the only argument against the Ottawa accord, it would be worth signing, since a small net benefit is better than no benefit.

However, the current convention suffers more significantly in that it makes no distinction between mines with an unlimited shelf life—and hence of unlimited danger to civilians—and "smarter" mines that are designed to self-destruct within a fixed period and thus pose a far smaller danger to civilians. The United States generally uses the latter. And in the Korean Peninsula, the United States, together with South Korea, has an apparently logical reason to want land mines—the presence of a million-man army across the demilitarized zone (DMZ), controlled by a regime that remains extremist and committed at least in theory to the reunification of the peninsula, by force if necessary.

While the Ottawa Convention is flawed, as a practical matter it would be unlikely to cause the United States any harm. In Korea, allied forces are now much stronger than those of North Korea, obviating much of the earlier need for land mines. And to the extent that a weapon whose effects are like those of land mines is still needed, the United States and South Korea now have technology allowing for rapid activation of minefields in a way that is consistent with the convention. But treaties should be asked to do more than simply not cause harm, and the Ottawa treaty it is not particularly well designed. An accord banning all types of persistent mines (antipersonnel and antivehicular) while allowing self-deactivating mines would be more sound in military terms and more beneficial in humanitarian terms.

Signing the Ottawa accord might gain the United States diplomatic capital for other arms control and security efforts of more importance to American interests. Indeed, treaties of marginal benefit to the United States and its allies can and should be supported if they are soundly conceived and important to other countries. But bad treaties should not be endorsed simply to curry favor. The Ottawa Convention would not do the United States significant harm, but it is not a very logical or well-crafted accord. It would be much better to design a different treaty than to settle for this one.

Regional Military Balances: The Taiwan Strait, South Asia, and the Middle East

Conventional arms control contributed, if belatedly and rather modestly, to ending the cold war. The Conventional Forces in Europe (CFE) Treaty helped to stabilize and defuse the NATO-Warsaw Pact military competition in its most crucial geographic theater and in its most expensive form of armament. There may be some room for applying similar concepts elsewhere. However, doing so is difficult; as argued below, Korea may be the only theater where a similar approach would make sense today.

Three regions in which conventional arms control is difficult to employ, at least in any broad and enduring way, are the Taiwan Strait, South Asia, and the Middle East–Persian Gulf area. In all three cases, fundamental strategic realities argue against formal and far-ranging accords. To put it simply, the two (or more) sides to the military balance in each region fundamentally disagree about what that balance should be. The key organizing concept of parity, which was so critical in the CFE Treaty, is not an option that will be widely accepted in these cases. Hence, while modest and temporary measures to build confidence or reduce the risks of an inadvertent war or an arms race may be useful, sweeping curbs on conventional armaments are not.

In the Taiwan Strait, the People's Republic of China (PRC) clearly would like to have as many credible offensive military options as possible, and Taiwan naturally opposes that idea. China's military is several times the size of Taiwan's, and its equipment inventories are typically three to five times as large.[26] China will therefore hardly be inclined to accept equal weapons or personnel ceilings in most categories of equipment. More broadly, without fundamental political changes in China, which would probably make the PRC-Taiwan conflict moot, China will not accept any arms regime that permanently precludes it from having the capacity to seize Taiwan. Nor will it agree to an accord that denies it coercive power in the form of missiles of the type it fired near Taiwan in 1995 and 1996 to signal its displeasure with Taiwan's efforts to raise its international profile (by pursuing a seat in the UN and diplomatic relations with a number of countries, among other things). Indeed, China will probably also insist on retaining the option of conducting larger missile strikes—possibly even directed against land targets—or of maintaining a naval blockade of some type.[27] It also sees itself as an ascendant power, and despite numerous underappreciated economic difficulties, it is indeed likely to grow substantially in power in the twenty-first century.[28] Even those who believe that the PRC would almost surely never conduct an attack against Taiwan under currently plausible political circumstances should recognize that Beijing's leadership probably wants Taipei to worry that it might. China's leaders fear that otherwise Taiwan could declare independence without feeling any serious deterrent to doing so, an outcome that would be fundamentally unacceptable in Beijing.[29] An accord ensuring anything remotely approaching parity would be a nonstarter.

Accords based on concepts other than parity might in theory be possible, but they would require the two sides to accept a specific power asymmetry for an extended period of time. In a dynamic setting in which each country is modernizing its economy and its military quickly, it is difficult to imagine what type of power balance both would find desirable enough to codify. This is especially true given the fact that China wishes its military capability to appear at least somewhat threatening to Taiwan at the same time that Taiwan considers such a state of affairs unacceptable.

Some restraints on arms sales to China still make sense. Rather than lift restrictions, as it has been considering, the European Union should stick with the policy of maintaining controls on advanced weapons transfers to the PRC that its members and the United States have followed since Tiananmen Square. Some limits on high-tech weapons can reduce the odds that China will risk a confrontation with the United States in the Taiwan Strait. So in this narrow sense, arms control—on the supply side—can be helpful. But such restraints cannot be expected to prevent China from pursuing, and probably obtaining, a substantial overall military edge over Taiwan.[30]

In South Asia, the problem is similar. India possesses conventional military superiority over Pakistan—its edge is roughly two to one by most major measures—and it is hard to believe, given its size and regional aspirations, that New Delhi would commit itself to accept nothing more than parity in the future.[31] It also has a wary eye on China, further reducing the chances that it would ever accept parity with Pakistan. Despite the fact that Pakistan's nuclear weapons now make territorial conquest or regime change far less feasible, even as an extreme policy recourse, India will probably want to retain the ability to conduct strikes against terrorist training camps within Pakistan and perhaps will want to preserve other limited military options. At a time when its own seat of government has been threatened in the recent past by terrorists with some links (direct or indirect) to Pakistan and when India continues to view retention of Kashmir as critical to its core stability as a nation, it will not sacrifice its superiority. The stakes are too high for it to give up offensive options despite the associated risks, including nuclear escalation. At the same time, it is doubtful that Pakistan would be willing to codify its conventional inferiority, symbolically and legally confirming its status as a lesser power than India. Thus it is unlikely that a major structural conventional arms control arrangement can be negotiated.[32]

In the Middle East and Persian Gulf, the problem is more complex. There are many more actors. Some rely on the size of their armed forces for protection, others on the quality of their armed forces, and still others on the United States. Moreover, some countries are in effect part of more than one military balance: Syria, for example, keeps one eye on Israel, but the other on other states in the region.[33]

It is difficult to use arms control to construct a stable military balance in such a complex setting even if all parties agree that they want peace and are prepared to forswear their ability to launch offensive military operations.[34] For one thing, two sides with equal forces will not necessarily fight to a standstill, and historically, smaller foes often beat larger ones, due to the advantages of surprise, maneuvers, smart tactics, psychological shock, and other factors.[35] In such situations there is probably no way to guarantee peace through arms control. In addition, in a region of potentially shifting alliances it is unclear which countries or groups of countries should be balanced against which (especially in the Persian Gulf). Finally, attempting arms control for the Arab-Israeli conflict could raise some tough questions that regional countries might do better not to highlight with their own populations at present. For example, should Egypt view Israel as a potential enemy or not, and vice versa? Should the combined forces of Syria and Egypt be balanced in some way against those of Israel? And how, if at all, could Israel's qualitative military advantage be recognized or factored into any accord (not to mention its nuclear weapons capability)? Although Israel and the United States might argue that it should not be considered, the Arab neighbors of Israel might feel differently.

These conclusions do not preclude a number of specific confidence-building measures and forms of agreed, if usually informal and temporary, restraint on certain arms acquisitions and deployments. For example, by improving communication during crises, hotline arrangements are generally useful as confidence-building measures. They can be improved in South Asia and introduced in the Taiwan Strait, as can military-to-military contacts that create some transparency and trust when forces come into virtual contact with each other routinely. Pullback zones can be useful in places where distances are short and warning times are minimal, as in the Arab-Israeli theater. Protocols on avoiding incidents that call for prenotification of missile launches and other such safety and reassurance measures are generally good ideas too.[36] Avoiding inadvertent war is important, virtually regardless of broader strategic and military realities.

Other limited steps may sometimes help too, even when broad accords are impractical. For example, China's continued buildup of short-range missiles near the Taiwan Strait may have become counterproductive for both sides. For Taiwan, it translates into growing vulnerability—even if the vulnerability is more a reflection of China's ability to inflict harm on civilian populations or otherwise cause terror than to destroy Taiwanese military targets. For China, there are also costs, most likely in the form of increased U.S. sales of missile defense systems to Taiwan. Such arms would be extremely troubling to Beijing, less perhaps for their military significance than for the greater level of U.S.-Taiwan cooperation that would be implied, especially in areas such as command and control and missile launch early warning.[37]

Some sort of explicit or even tacit agreement to slow down the dynamic may make sense. For example, Taiwan could agree to only a modest upgrade in its missile defense systems in the coming years if China will avoid future buildups. However, this approach, if not pursued carefully, involves dangers. Were Taiwan to forgo any and all missile defense capabilities while China agreed only to freeze deployments of missiles near Taiwan, the PRC could reverse its decision and redeploy missiles to the vicinity of the strait, violating the accord, much more quickly than Taiwan could obtain and learn to use better missile defenses.[38] But by contrast, if Taiwan had upgraded its missile defenses somewhat and was disinclined to spend the money to improve them further, a limited and nonpermanent deal might work.

In South Asia, where the economies of the two main protagonists are still severely challenged by problems of domestic poverty, tacit or temporary accords to limit the pace of military modernization could be considered. But it would be tough to make these work well, since neither side is prepared to stop improving its arms and since India, with its impressive rate of economic growth in recent times, will surely want to reinforce its quantitative edge against Pakistan and bolster its sense of security with respect to China by making further qualitative enhancements to its forces. And a vaguely worded or poorly understood accord on slowing modernization can lead to acrimony if one side pushes up against—or over—the intended limits. This dynamic can actually worsen relations, despite the best intentions of the restraint agreement.

If clarity could be achieved—for example, by setting a numerical limit on acquisition and deployment of fourth-generation fighter fleets (which would likely require Pakistan to make the difficult decision to formally accept at least some degree of military inferiority vis-à-vis India)—there could be some modest yet real benefits, at least in financial terms. Similarly, force pullbacks could be considered in and around Kashmir. But again, one must worry about unintended consequences. Were India to agree to pullbacks in the expectation that Pakistan would clamp down on terrorist groups in its territory but later found out that Pakistan had failed to deliver, India's redeployment of forces closer to the line of control could actually produce a tenser situation than if the pullback had never occurred in the first place.

In the Persian Gulf, some rough limits on the size of arsenals or on the dollar volume of arms sales to the region could be a useful check on the tendency of states in the region to overmilitarize.[39] For example, a general understanding that no country would import more than $1 billion to $2 billion in arms each year might limit expenditures without causing any strategic imbalances—even though it would be important to recognize that it would not ensure regional stability.[40] So could restraints on exporting certain advanced technologies like cruise missiles, stealth aircraft, or ballistic missiles to the region.[41] Given the petrodollars in the hands of regional governments, Western weapons suppliers tend to be too ready to grant their wishes, while prestige and security considerations sometimes drive these governments to spend more on arms than their budgets can easily afford. But regimes restricting such sales are difficult to formally implement.[42] And given Iran's new status in the post-Saddam era as the clear regional heavyweight (given the size of its population), as well as its nuclear programs, it is conceivable that the Gulf states will someday have a good reason for spending large sums on high-tech naval and air forces to protect themselves.

Ultimately, conventional arms control arrangements may be able to reduce the chances of inadvertent war, reduce the costs of military preparations for war, and otherwise meet traditional arms control criteria. But expectations must be kept modest, and the potential for counterproductive arms control measures must be continually kept in mind.

Turning to the Korean Peninsula, although the nuclear issue is the most acute security threat posed by North Korea (DPRK), it is conventional forces that have been at the heart of the half-century-long military standoff there.[43] Moreover, conventional forces are the ones that consume most of the country's military resources, weighing down its economy. This makes the issue of conventional forces much different than in the Taiwan Strait or South Asia, where military expenditures are not nearly so egregiously large a percentage of GDP. And it is conventional force reductions that, if properly carried out, can give hope to North Korea and help provide the economic foundation it needs to abandon its reliance on bribes and blackmail to keep itself afloat.[44] Unlike in the Middle East and Persian Gulf, conventional arms cuts in the Korean Peninsula would be relatively simple to conceptualize because there are only two straightforward military blocs at issue. And also unlike most other cases, a relatively simple accord based on the principle of equal percentage reductions may seem fair to the parties involved—largely because neither appears to be maneuvering for an offensive war-winning capability.

What type of conventional arms reduction agreement could be significant enough in scope to free up large amounts of resources? How could it be made verifiable, so that the United States and South Korea (ROK) would know that they were not being tricked, and made to have a militarily stabilizing effect on all parties concerned? The allies would need to be sure that Pyongyang would not feel emboldened to attack by any cutback in forces; Pyongyang in turn would need to be reassured that it was not being duped into letting down its guard and making itself vulnerable to preemptive attack by the allies. Given North Korea's limited knowledge of arms control and virtual lack of experience in the field, that will take some doing.

Consider for example a 50 percent reduction in heavy weaponry on the Korean Peninsula, backed up by on-site verification. This type of accord could be modeled after the NATO–Warsaw Pact Conventional Forces in Europe Treaty, which placed clear numerical constraints on holdings of heavy weaponry and allowed routine as well as challenge inspections to verify that countries were not exceeding their allotted totals. U.S. forces based in Korea would be counted against ROK holdings; U.S. forces elsewhere would not be. Since potential American reinforcements would be substantial in number, North Korea might insist that most of the allied reductions would have to come from South Korea's holdings to be truly meaningful. This approach should be acceptable to Washington and Seoul. However, Pyongyang might push the other way and try to maximize U.S. reductions, hoping to gradually reduce the American presence on the peninsula; that alternative would have to be opposed, especially in light of the fact that America's already small standing forces on the peninsula are already being downsized from roughly 38,000 uniformed personnel to 25,000.

In any event, under such an accord, forces near the DMZ would have to be cut back proportionately on both sides, just as with the CFE Treaty, which imposed certain sublimits on forces within certain geographic zones. But forces near the DMZ would not have to be drawn down to zero. Since North Korea's ability to deter any allied attack lies largely in its ability to hold Seoul hostage, it is simply not realistic to think that North Korea would pull its forces back from the DMZ entirely. Indeed, it would be just as well to keep substantial allied forces near the DMZ to enhance allied forward defense capability, meaning that it will probably be necessary to live with a substantial percentage of DPRK forces relatively close to the DMZ.

Like the CFE Treaty, the treaty proposed here could be phased in over a period of about three years. Once implemented, it would remain in force indefinitely.

The CFE Treaty held both parties to the same quantitative limits on heavy weaponry. But as noted, given the strength of their present military posture, Washington and Seoul could offer even easier terms to North Korea, suggesting 50 percent cuts in heavy weaponry on both sides of the DMZ. North Korea would retain a certain (though reduced) quantitative advantage over the allies but at lower levels of armament for both sides. The United States and South Korea would still have an enormous advantage in weapons quality, in military assets that are not counted within the CFE framework (such as advanced reconnaissance systems), and in U.S. reinforcement capability.

In theory, the allies might choose to meet their obligations under the proposed treaty by cutting ROK forces only, leaving the modestly sized U.S. capability in South Korea (including weapons in storage there) unaffected. But it would probably be wiser, as a sign of good faith, to make at least symbolic cuts in American weaponry (or at least to codify by treaty the ongoing reductions in U.S. forces). At the same time, Washington and

Seoul must make clear that they categorically reject North Korea's traditional demand that conventional force reductions be used as a vehicle for pushing U.S. forces off the peninsula.[45]

Treaties defined in these terms are difficult to negotiate. A number of thorny issues must be resolved, such as whether to count weapons-capable training aircraft as combat aircraft and where to define the cut-off between artillery and generally smaller mortars, which are not limited. It is also necessary to agree on how excess weapons will be destroyed and to work out verification procedures. Fortunately, the CFE experience provides considerable background for handling these and other matters. If North Korea wished, it clearly could seek guidance from Russia on how to draw from the CFE model without prejudice to its interests.[46]

The CFE Treaty does not limit military manpower, and neither, presumably, would a Conventional Forces in Korea (CFK) accord. In principle, if North Korea wished, it could keep all its troops whose heavy equipment had been destroyed, give them rifles instead, and turn them into infantry soldiers. This would be a violation of the spirit, though not the letter, of the accord we propose—less for its military significance than for its economic consequences. If North Korea kept the huge army it now fields, which consumes at least 25 percent of the nation's GDP and thus is extremely debilitating economically, the country's prospects for economic recovery would probably diminish substantially. It is not practical to count troop totals using reconnaissance assets, so there is little to be done about this potential shortcoming of a CFK treaty, except to use economic analysis to try to convince Pyongyang that it would be hurting itself to keep a military of the current size. Fortunately for the allies, even if North Korea failed to make 50 percent troop cuts, its military capabilities would remain quite constrained by such an accord (as well as by its failing economy and backward technology).

How can the United States and the ROK be confident that any arms cuts they make under an agreement with North Korea will do more good than harm? If a reduction were to create holes in allied defenses, that could tempt North Korea to attack even if its own forces were also scaled back. But in fact, even a Conventional Forces in Korea treaty that imposed comparable percentage cuts in weapons holdings on both sides would be stabilizing. Allied forces would remain at least as strong relative to those of North Korea, and they would have sufficient power in place to hold off an invasion even in the early going.[47] This conclusion can be supported by a combination of methods, including comparing the weapons of the two sides, estimating how much combat power is required to defend a given length of front, and conducting a dynamic simulation of combat. All of these considerations suggest strongly that a 50 percent cut in forces would serve allied security interests in Korea while also potentially spurring deep reductions in North Korean military spending, which would be needed for any economic reform agenda to succeed there.

Conclusion

Beyond the U.S.-Russian or European theater, traditional arms reduction concepts often have limited applicability. Among the world's major regional hot spots, broad and formal accords mandating conventional force reductions are likely to be useful only in Korea. But this conclusion is not entirely discouraging. If conventional arms reductions can make a meaningful difference in even one major case, that would represent an enormous contribution. And in other places, confidence-building measures or limited and specific agreements on restraints may reduce the chances that a crisis will escalate—or at least save money that might otherwise be wasted on an arms race. The challenge is to use arms control as a tool where appropriate but to avoid it when traditional techniques cannot provide much help.

Moreover, some types of weapons, such as certain specialized small arms, are so lethal that controlling them is desirable even if it is difficult. These weapons are hard to control, given their size and the large number of places in which they can be produced. But by combining various measures—tighter domestic legislation on arms sales, coordinated among participating countries; codes of conduct regarding when and to whom to sell; and clampdowns on the financial assets of undesirable groups buying or selling arms—the international community can make a difference, at least in some conflicts, at least at the margin. Given the severity of the human costs associated with the use of conventional arms in civil conflicts—and the degree to which failed states can provide a haven and resources for terrorists—even imperfect efforts have value.

CHAPTER 7

Conclusion: The Future of Arms Control

During the cold war, arms control aimed to constrain the superpowers in their race for military superiority and to reduce the huge financial burden of preparing for the possibility of war. It fostered contact and communication between the leaders and military officers of the opposing blocs. And by reinforcing the taboo on the use of nuclear weapons and containing nuclear proliferation, it aimed to minimize the damage from any war that might ultimately occur.

That emphasis on preventing nuclear proliferation remains important today. In addition, cold war arms control concepts can still contribute to achieving other goals, such as reducing conventional weaponry on the Korean Peninsula, banning antisatellite weapons that would create debris in orbit, and creating "zero options" in certain geographic regions that prohibit entire classes of weaponry, such as nuclear armaments. But otherwise, the geostrategic environment has shifted so much and the technological realities have changed so radically that new guideposts are needed. An age in which terrorists and rogues—normally weak actors—are empowered by the spread of massively destructive technology demands a new approach to arms control.

Arms control is imperative for contending with a dangerous world. But it should not always, or even most frequently, be understood as a laborious legal process, its most prominent cold war manifestation. Properly defined, it is any coordinated international action to constrain the development, production, and use of dangerous technologies. This does not mean that highly detailed treaties should be shunned, only that they are rarely likely to be necessary or desirable. On that point, opponents of traditional arms control have been right, even as they have categorically opposed too many useful treaty concepts and otherwise failed to develop a broad new arms control strategy.

Arms control, defined this way, remains vitally important. Current controls on biological technologies are entirely inadequate in a world in which advances in microbiology are occurring quickly. Nuclear materials remain too prevalent and inadequately secured in Russia, and they are far too laxly guarded in many other places. With Pakistan, India, North Korea, and Iran all making varying degrees of progress toward building nuclear arsenals in recent years, international support for the Nuclear Non-Proliferation Treaty has lost much of the momentum it gained in the early to mid-1990s. The conditions that give rise to terrorism or that help terrorist organizations find the resources and refuge they need—failed states, civil conflict, illicit trade in gems and timber and other sources of income that permit easy access to small arms—are prevalent in too much of the developing world. They also cause huge harm to the populations directly affected.

Arms control should focus on preventing terrorist groups and extremist regimes from gaining access to the world's most dangerous weapons. It must tighten controls on nuclear and biological technologies in particular. It should also work to deprive terrorist groups and extremist militias of resources and sanctuaries—a goal that leads logically to focusing on failed states and civil conflict, serious problems in their own right that involve especially large segments of the developing world. Arms control is never a sufficient tool for addressing these challenges; it is only occasionally even the main tool. But it is frequently important and useful.

Arms control solutions to some problems may involve formal treaty-based approaches if they are meaningful and verifiable. Generally these will be multilateral accords, not bilateral ones. At least as often, however, they will involve individual countries' coordinated use of national legislation and other action to achieve the desired result—as, for example, with controlling biological technologies or trade in arms through the Proliferation Security Initiative. Another set of useful approaches can involve a temporary restraint on weapons development—as with certain types of antisatellite weapons—that individual countries would adopt to encourage similar restraint from others. They can also employ policy instruments such as cooperative threat reduction programs in dangerous places outside the original U.S.-Russian context. All of these approaches should be thought of as arms control because all are systematic, cooperative attempts by a community of countries to constrain the development and use of dangerous technologies.

Certain kinds of treaties should be not only deemphasized but avoided. For example, new, detailed arms accords such as those that place limits on U.S. and Russian offensive or defensive strategic nuclear capabilities reinforce old ways of thinking about strategic dynamics and can take up too much of the time of policymakers in the executive branch and in Congress. Broad conventional arms accords for the Persian Gulf, South Asia, or the Taiwan Strait cannot be designed in a way that both stabilizes the military balance and respects the main security priorities of the principal parties in those areas (though more limited agreements may have value). Any biological weapons accord that even indirectly helped authoritarian or aggressive states obtain dangerous technologies would likely cause more harm than good, as would one that encroached on biodefense research; for that reason the verification protocol to the Biological Weapons Convention proposed in 2001 is imperfect and should be improved. Any outright ban on deploying weapons in space would be unverifiable and impractical, as would any eventual accord on abolishing nuclear weapons. And the current land mine convention, while unlikely to cause the United States real military harm, is not designed in such a way as to do enough good.

Constraining the conventional military strength of the great powers should not be a goal of arms control. Unlike in the cold war era, today the risk of an arms race between major states is negligible—except, perhaps, between China and the United States over the Taiwan Strait, a possibility that lies outside the realm of most forms of arms control because both would want to be able to win any war that might ensue. Nor is the current size of the military forces of the great powers generally a threat to the international system. Some would argue otherwise, especially in the aftermath of the unilateralist American decision to go to war against Saddam Hussein. But if the worst trangression of the United States is to lead the overthrow of Saddam Hussein, one of the world's worst tyrants, after having obtained only partial international legitimacy for the operation, it should be clear that America's actions are hardly the precursor of a reckless imperialism. Future formal constraints on its actions, to the extent they are prudent, should be considered through political and legal processes (mostly on a case-by-case basis), not through arms control limits on its power.

If anything, the world would be well served if more major Western countries develop stronger militaries. Such a change could produce a more effective and meaningful check on U.S. unilateralism than arms control can offer. If more countries had significant militaries, more of them could have a significant influence in key decisions regarding the use of force.

It is important not to overload the arms control agenda. Pursuing agreements that deliver only marginal benefit simply to create momentum for disarmament and to embellish the existing infrastructure of global governance often is counterproductive. It distracts busy policymakers from the key arms control priorities and forces them to devote a great deal of time to understanding treaties of limited importance to ensure that they will do the United States no long-term harm. Worst of all, it risks discrediting arms control in the eyes of many key constituencies, especially in the United States but also elsewhere, by reinforcing the argument that arms control is an ideological, utopian crusade.

It is critical to view arms control as an integral part of the overall security policy of the United States and other countries, not as an alternative to more assertive traditional forms of national security policy. Some arms control proponents may aspire to global governance or the abolishment of nuclear arms, but they should not harbor any illusions about the practicality of achieving those objectives—or expect others to see them even as desirable goals.

The most important formal accomplishment of arms control—the 1968 Nuclear Non-Proliferation Treaty—needs to be undergirded by a new strategy. It is not practical to hold the world's nuclear powers to their original promise to eliminate nuclear weapons anytime in the foreseeable future. But neither is it right or reasonable to expect the world's nuclear have-nots to accept second-class status indefinitely, especially if their national security seems to demand a formidable deterrent of some sort. Offering them civilian nuclear benefits and technology is not a good enough substitute. Nor is it even a good idea, unless carefully constrained and accompanied by robust monitoring.

The old NPT bargain does not need to be explicitly discarded—doing so would probably cause more harm than good—but it must be thoroughly renovated. Most countries do not benefit from having nuclear weapons and recognize that fact. Most are not at serious risk of attack. For others, nuclear weapons could not credibly prevent the kinds of attack that they would most likely suffer. Some realize that pursuing nuclear weapons might inflame tense political relationships in their neighborhoods and make war more rather than less likely. And most benefit from participating in a regime that, in exchange for their forgoing nuclear weapons, reassures them their neighbors will forgo them too.

That said, the United States feels, probably correctly, that having nuclear weapons improves its own security and that of its allies. The other permanent members of the UN Security Council, as well as Israel, and, apparently, India, Pakistan, and North Korea, also desire their own deterrents. If the United States hopes to prevent more countries from reaching the same conclusion—and ideally to persuade some countries now possessing nuclear weapons capabilities to abandon them—it needs to propose a credible alternative. And that alternative must be seen as an integral part of its arms control strategy, not something separate.

During the cold war, the United States and its allies organized security communities based on the concept of collective security. This concept was most apparent in the NATO alliance, but it was also critical in the U.S.-Japan and U.S.–South Korea alliances. It sent a message to the world that the United States would consider any attack on its major allies tantamount to an attack on itself. Collective security arrangements have not always worked: the Central Treaty Organization (CENTO) and Southeast Asia Treaty Organization (SEATO), which were designed to help provide security to countries such as Iran and Vietnam in the early days of the cold war, fell short. But on balance security guarantees issued by the United States and other Western powers have been seen as quite serious by most countries involved. For evidence, one need note only how many eastern European countries have wished to join NATO in recent years. Admittedly, the primary purpose of many is to integrate themselves more fully into the West, economically and politically, but security concerns have influenced the thinking of a number as well. Similarly, during the cold war a number of countries in Europe as well as Japan, South Korea, and Taiwan refrained from developing their own nuclear weapons in part because of their confidence in the collective security guarantees they were given. Collective security has also been applied effectively beyond Europe and East Asia, the failures of SEATO and CENTO notwithstanding. For example, while the United States does not have alliances with the Persian Gulf members of the Gulf Cooperation Council, it acts as if it does—as it has proven clearly since 1990.

As a key part of arms control strategy, the United States and its allies should build on this experience to offer a broad but focused vision of collective security to the world in general. No country should be asked to accept a permanent lack of security because of its non-nuclear status. Rather, the United States and like-minded powers should offer guarantees to countries that need help to ensure their national security, so long as they forgo weapons of mass destruction. Any such offer must, of course, include certain additional requirements of its recipients. They should govern themselves democratically, maintain civilian control of the military, behave peacefully toward neighbors, and seek to cooperate in solving regional and global security problems (such as by participating in peacekeeping missions or regional diplomacy efforts); they should also have demonstrated solid compliance with nonproliferation objectives. If they cannot immediately meet all these conditions, they must, at a minimum, be moving in the right direction.

This positive cooperative security vision is different from the types of security pledges that might have to be considered for countries posing specific problems to the international community. For example, it may be necessary for the United States to agree to a regional security pact in Northeast Asia if it is to convince North Korea to relinquish its nuclear arms. The latter can be tolerated provided that North Korea's behavior at home or abroad does not worsen badly and that the DPRK does not itself engage in unprovoked aggression against its neighbors (or its own people). But such conditional and more limited "negative" security pledges not to attack adversaries are fundamentally different from the type of pact that the United States should envision for a broader collective security community in the future.

Just like the Nuclear Non-Proliferation Treaty's promise of eventual nuclear disarmament, this is a long-term vision—though unlike the disarmament promise, it is one that can be achieved. It is not a prescription for an immediate or even ultimate global collective security community. The United States already has some seventy treaty partners (twenty-five in NATO, more than thirty in the Rio Pact, at least ten in the Persian Gulf, and a handful in East Asia); it does not need to double the number overnight. Nor would it. The criteria proposed are sufficiently demanding that most countries outside the current system could not quickly become eligible. As a practical matter, these absolute requirements may have to be relaxed in some cases, such as Ukraine or Saudi Arabia. But the United States and its allies could be patient and demanding before pledging their own troops' lives to help defend most of the world's countries, as opposed to merely pledging not to attack them. Even if collective security is a long-term goal, it is a realistic one toward which progress can be made over time, and a key component of a successful arms control strategy.

The Path Ahead: Specific Technologies and Specific Proposals

Controlling dangerous technologies more effectively requires a broad set of initiatives. To prevent the misuse of biotechnology, policymakers should begin by more vigorously encouraging other countries to toughen and coordinate their domestic laws regulating and enhancing the safety and security of research activities. A strong verification protocol for the Biological Weapons Convention should also be pursued. The current proposal should be improved to make it clear that a narrowly construed compliance will not be enough for countries to gain easy access to dangerous biological technologies. Countries will need a clear record of good compliance with nonproliferation obligations, peaceful resolution of any conflicts, democratic government, and transparency in biological research before enjoying full privileges in the trade in advanced microbiological materials.

Arms control has more to offer in the nuclear sphere. Some classical arms control concepts still have utility here. The likely benefits of U.S. ratification of the Comprehensive Test Ban Treaty are compelling, and the downsides are minimal. Treaty critics are right to argue that even if the United States ratifies the treaty it likely will not change the minds of many leaders in countries such as North Korea about the desirability of pursuing nuclear arms. But it will strengthen the U.S. position with other law-abiding nations when Washington attempts to apply pressure or impose penalties on proliferant regimes, and it will give the United States more political capital to promote nonproliferation in other ways. The CTBT should also make it harder for countries to test nuclear weapons, including advanced weapons that might be deployed on long-range missiles, given the pressure and penalties that could result. At the same time, the U.S. nuclear stockpile can be reliably maintained indefinitely without testing, and the prospect of developing important new military tools through testing of new types of warheads is poor in any event. Even if domestic support of the CTBT remains elusive, the United States can gain many of the CTBT's benefits by simply refraining from nuclear testing. But the argument against testing is strong and enduring enough that treaty ratification would be greatly preferable.

Other steps needed to strengthen nuclear security are outside the classical province of arms control. The United States, with its G-8 partners, must expand its cooperative threat reduction program. It may not need to spend $30 billion more on the enterprise, as is often advocated, but the case appears strong for allocating an additional $20 billion over the coming five to ten years. And the United States should not simply make a greater effort to tighten controls over Russian nuclear materials; in addition, much of the increase should go to expanding efforts to secure nuclear materials in military, civilian, and research programs worldwide.

The Proliferation Security Initiative has a compelling logic, invoking widely accepted arms control standards to build support for coercive action against dangerous regimes and proliferation-related behavior. It should be broadened to include more participating countries and strengthened to provide an international legal basis for more muscular enforcement of arms control on the high seas and in international airspace.

To give the nonproliferation regime stronger teeth, all states with nuclear technology programs should be required to adopt the International Atomic Energy Agency's Additional Protocol, which permits more intrusive inspections beyond sites where large-scale, declared nuclear activities occur. These obligations should not be viewed as optional, whether or not a state is currently a party to the NPT and whether or not it wishes to continue to be. As an adjunct, an international whistle-blower program should be created to protect scientists willing to share information about illicit nuclear or biological weapons activities in their home countries.

In addition, the NPT should be formally reinterpreted to prohibit production of highly enriched uranium and construction of new facilities for separating plutonium throughout the world. Ideally, non-nuclear states should also be prohibited from acquiring technologies to enrich uranium at all (even up to low U-235 levels, which are not suitable for nuclear bombs). As an incentive for compliance, nuclear states should guarantee them a nuclear fuel supply. If that approach does not prove feasible or if policymakers conclude that pushing too hard for such a discriminatory approach would poison the waters for a useful compromise, the United States should pursue an alternative approach requiring multinational ownership of all new enrichment facilities. The multinational ownership consortiums should include only countries with records of adherence to nonproliferation accords. (This requirement should apply even to facilities in the territory of the nuclear powers.) This would add transparency and complicate efforts to use enrichment facilities for weapons purposes.

Such an approach should replace the proposed Fissile Material Cut-off Treaty. The latter covers only materials purportedly developed for weapons purposes and therefore has huge loopholes.

States outside the NPT (even India and Israel) should not be assisted with their nuclear energy programs. States that acquire any nuclear-related technologies while within the NPT but later attempt to withdraw should not be viewed as legitimately owning those technologies. Indeed, not only should the international community insist on the return of such technologies (and potentially threaten military strikes to destroy any assets not returned), it should open up the possibility of more far-reaching and asymmetric punishment up to and including regime change.

These steps will greatly improve monitoring and early warning—but the international community, beginning with the United States and Europe, must go beyond those measures to enforcement. In the case of extremist states with a clear history of aggression, nondemocratic government, ruthless internal practices, and noncompliance with nonproliferation obligations—especially nuclear and biological—enforcement should be especially tough. Extremely tight economic sanctions, potentially followed by the use of military force—either to surgically destroy nuclear facilities when feasible and practical or to overthrow the regime when necessary—should be seriously considered if the offending government does not demonstrate a sharp and clear change in attitude.

The international community will often have trouble deciding which regimes are so dangerous that they warrant extreme action and even more trouble deciding when to declare that diplomatic efforts have failed. Purely mechanistic and automatic rules of the road for when to coerce, strike, or overthrow sovereign governments might be desirable if all regimes were alike and if competing priorities were absent, but that is never the case, making a flexible approach necessary. Nonetheless, by agreeing in principle that sharp steps are warranted in an age of terror and weapons proliferation—and not only as a last resort chronologically—the international community can improve its readiness to act when necessary. In turn, it can also enhance the credibility of its threats so that crises requiring extreme measures become less common than they might otherwise be.

Conclusion

Because most of the problems involved in confronting dangerous technology cannot be handled by the United States alone, arms control—systematic multilateral efforts to control the development, production, and use of dangerous technologies and associated weaponry—is as imperative as ever. Nevertheless, arms control needs desperately to change, in keeping with the fundamental upheaval in the international security environment since the end of the cold war.

Thinking grounded in cold war geopolitics must be left behind. Limiting arms competition among superpowers should no longer be the overriding objective of coordinated international efforts to control dangerous technology. Instead, the world needs to use arms control whenever it can to try to keep the most dangerous technologies out of the hands of the most dangerous actors, especially terrorist groups and extremist states.

To avoid making arms control a narrow means of advancing only Western security, policymakers also must wrestle to the extent possible with the security problems of the developing world. Indeed, these often become Western security problems too, given the nexus between failed states and terrorism. Recognizing that in much of the world, the real weapons of mass destruction are small arms and the conflict and chaos that they can exacerbate, they need to do whatever is feasible—despite the difficulties of the task—to limit access to such weaponry. (They must also seek to mitigate such conflict in other ways, such as through diplomacy, economic instruments, and in some cases humanitarian military intervention.)

The international community should think of arms control less as the diametric opposite of coercion. In many cases it goes hand in glove with coercion, helping to establish the legal and political predicate for muscular action. Policymakers need to recognize that even the best arms control arrangements can fail and accordingly design accords that provide the maximum advance warning possible so that coercive measures can be contemplated against dangerous states that violate those accords.

The consensus on cold war arms control rightly emphasized the need to bring defense and arms control policy into careful harmony. During the cold war, that meant ensuring that arms control and military *preparations* would be mutually supportive; now it means that arms control and coercive *action* must be just as closely and carefully linked. Arms control incentives must reflect regional security needs, which predominate today. That means arms control must also be linked to broader strategy involving the tools of security guarantees and alliance formation. There is much for all nations to revisit and rethink. But a new consensus is possible. It is imperative.

APPENDIX

Arms Control Treaties and Other Accords

Contents

This appendix was prepared by Adriana Lins de Albuquerque.

Nuclear Non-Proliferation Treaty

Treaty on the Non-Proliferation of Nuclear Weapons, opened for signature on July 1, 1968, and entered into force on March 5, 1970

Provisions

The Nuclear Non-Proliferation Treaty (NPT) defines "nuclear weapons states" as states that have "manufactured and exploded a nuclear weapon or other nuclear explosive devices prior to 1 January 1967." The five nuclear weapons states acknowledged by the treaty—the United States, Russia, the United Kingdom, France, and China—agree not to transfer nuclear weapons or nuclear explosive devices or to provide any recipient with the technology needed to process, use, or produce special fissile material. They also agree not to assist, encourage, or induce any non–nuclear weapons state to acquire or manufacture nuclear weapons or nuclear devices. Nuclear weapons states must nevertheless facilitate the exchange of information, equipment, and material related to peaceful uses of nuclear energy, such as power generation (as well as ensure, in the treaty's original interpretation, that benefits arising from the application of peaceful nuclear explosions be made available to non–nuclear weapons states that are party to the treaty). Finally, nuclear weapons states should continue to engage in negotiations aimed at curtailing a nuclear weapons arms race. The ultimate goal of such negotiations should be general and eventually complete nuclear disarmament.

Non–nuclear weapons states must refrain from acquiring or producing nuclear weapons or nuclear explosive devices. To ensure that no diversion from the peaceful use of nuclear materials occurs, non–nuclear weapons states must set up individual nuclear safeguard mechanisms in accordance with the provisions of the International Atomic Energy Agency (IAEA). As part of this process, all nuclear material belonging to a non–nuclear weapons state bound by the treaty must be declared to the IAEA and access to all civil facilities holding nuclear material must be provided to IAEA inspectors at their request.

Compliance

The United Nations Security Council and General Assembly have the authority to impose sanctions against member states that are in breach of the treaty. Sanctions can include suspension of assistance, voting privileges, or rights given as a function of the treaty as well as return of materials.

Status/Duration

The Nuclear Non-Proliferation Treaty was extended indefinitely on May 11, 1995. States party to the treaty have the right to withdraw from the treaty if they feel that "extraordinary events" related to issues regulated by the NPT are "jeopardizing the supreme interest of the country." As of September 2004, 189 states had ratified the NPT. North Korea announced its decision to withdraw from the treaty in 2002. India, Israel and Pakistan are the only states that are not, and never have been, parties to the treaty.

Web Resources

For the full text of the treaty, current status, the role of the IAEA in relation to the NPT, and developments at the most recent review conference, see the International Atomic Energy Agency (www.iaea.or.at/NewsCenter/Focus/Npt/index.shtml).

Comprehensive Nuclear Test Ban Treaty

Opened for signature on September 24, 1996; not in force as of October 2004

Provisions

Parties to the Comprehensive Nuclear Test Ban Treaty must refrain from carrying out any test explosions of nuclear weapons or any other nuclear explosion at any location under their control or jurisdiction. Underground facilities are considered to be within state jurisdiction. Member states may not cause, encourage, or in any way participate in the execution of any nuclear explosion or nuclear weapons explosion. These provisions apply to what some states refer to as "peaceful nuclear explosions" but not to nuclear-related activities that merely involve discharge of nuclear energy.

Compliance

When the treaty enters into force, a verification regime will be set up and implemented by the Comprehensive Test Ban Treaty Organization, the monitoring agency established under the treaty.

Status/Duration

Once in force, the treaty will be of unlimited duration. Member states are allowed to withdraw from the treaty if it is in their "supreme national interest" to do so. The treaty is not yet in force. In order for it to enter into force, forty-four countries that in 1996 possessed nuclear research or nuclear power reactors must ratify the treaty. Although 115 states had ratified the treaty as of September 2004, only thirty-two of the specified "nuclear-capable states" had done so. China, Colombia, the Democratic Republic of Congo, Egypt, Indonesia, Iran, Israel, the United States, and Vietnam have signed but not ratified the treaty. India, Pakistan, and North Korea have neither signed nor ratified the treaty.

Web Resources

For the full text of the treaty, a summary of its provisions, and a complete list of member states, see the Arms Control Association (www.armscontrol.org/factsheets/ctbtsig.asp).

Partial Test-Ban Treaty

Treaty Banning Nuclear Weapon Tests in the Atmosphere, in Outer Space and Under Water, opened for signature on August 5, 1963, and entered into force on October 10, 1963

Provisions

Member states vow to prohibit, prevent, and not to carry out most types of nuclear weapons test explosions or other nuclear explosions within their jurisdiction or control. They are also prohibited from carrying out such explosions in the atmosphere, outer space, and under water (including territorial waters and the high seas). In addition, they are not allowed to test in any other environment if it causes radioactive debris to reach outside the territorial borders of the state where the test is conducted. Member states should furthermore desist from causing, encouraging, or participating in carrying out nuclear weapons test explosions or other nuclear explosions in any of the environments referred to above.

Compliance

The PTBT does not specify a verification mechanism, but member states are expected to use their own national technical means to verify compliance.

Status/Duration

As of September 2004, 124 states had ratified the treaty. The United States is a party to the treaty; France and China are not. The treaty is of unlimited duration.

Web Resources

For the full text of the treaty, a chronology of events, and the complete list of member states, see the United Nations Department of Disarmament (disarmament2.un.org/TreatyStatus.nsf).

Seabed Treaty

Treaty on the Prohibition of the Emplacement of Nuclear Weapons and Other Weapons of Mass Destruction on the Seabed and the Ocean Floor and in the Subsoil Thereof, opened for signature on February 11, 1971, and entered into force on May 18, 1972

Provisions

Member states vow not to implant or place any nuclear weapons or any other types of weapons of mass destruction on the seabed or the ocean floor and in the subsoil thereof. The provisions, which should be upheld beyond a twelve-mile territorial zone, also apply to launching installations and facilities designed for storing, testing, or using nuclear weapons.

Compliance

Member states are to monitor each other's activities to ensure compliance with the treaty. A member state that has reasonable cause to question another member state's compliance can request verification. Once verification procedures have been completed, the state party that initiated the request should circulate a report to all member states. If doubt still remains as to whether a state party is in breach of the treaty, the matter is to be referred to the United Nations Security Council. The Security Council will deal with the issue in accordance with the provisions set forth in the United Nations Charter.

Status/Duration

As of September 2004, the treaty had been ratified by ninety-two states. The United States is a party to the treaty; France, Israel, and Pakistan are not. The treaty is of unlimited duration.

Web Resources

For the full text of the treaty and the complete list of member states, see the United Nations Department of Disarmament (disarmament2.un.org/TreatyStatus.nsf).

START I

Treaty between the United States of America and the Union of Soviet Socialist Republics on the Reduction and Limitation of Strategic Offensive Arms, signed on July 31, 1991, and entered into force on December 5, 1994

Provisions

Under START, the United States and the Soviet Union committed themselves to making reductions in their strategic nuclear forces for an initial period of seven years. The treaty sets limits on the number of intercontinental ballistic missiles (ICBMs), submarine-launched ballistic missiles (SLBMs), and heavy bombers. In addition, it sets limits on "accountable" warheads on ICBMs, SLBMs, heavy bombers, and heavy missiles, and it specifies the maximum ballistic missile throw-weight that each side may have.

Compliance

In order to verify compliance, START provides for numerous types of on-site inspections in addition to monitoring, exchange of detailed data, and an extensive notification regime.

Status/Duration

After having reached the arms reduction goals set forth for the initial seven-year period, the parties decided that the treaty would remain in force in order to verify continued compliance for a cumulative total of fifteen years. If the parties agree to do so, the treaty may be extended for successive five-year periods thereafter. The entering into force of SORT

(Treaty between the United States of American and the Russian Federation on Strategic Offensive Reductions) does not affect the need for the parties to abide by the provisions set forth by START, which remains in force without any additional amendments. The legal commitments of the Soviet Union were taken over by its successor states, Russia, Belarus, Kazakstan, and Ukraine, with the signing in 1992 of the Lisbon Protocol (Protocol to the Treaty between the United States of America and the Union of Soviet Socialist Republics on the Reduction and Limitation of Strategic Offensive Arms).

Web Resources

For the full text of the treaty and associated documents see the United States Department of State (www.state.gov/www/global/arms/starthtm/start/toc.html).

START II

Treaty between the United States of America and the Russian Federation on Further Reduction and Limitation of Strategic Offensive Arms, signed on January 3, 1993; not in force as of October 2004

Provisions

START II continues the nuclear arms reductions initiated by START I by calling for more stringent limits on the number of strategic nuclear weapons deployed. More specifically, the parties are to reduce their arsenals so that they have no more than 3,000 to 3,500 strategic nuclear warheads on intercontinental missiles (ICBMs), submarine-launched ballistic missiles (SLBMs), and heavy bombers by December 31, 2007. In addition, the parties are to deactivate all strategic nuclear delivery vehicles by removing their warheads or by taking other steps to the same effect by December 31, 2003. No multiple warheads (MIRVs) are allowed on ICBMs and no more than 1,700 to 1,750 of the strategic nuclear warheads may be deployed on SLBMs. Finally, all heavy Russian ICBMs must be destroyed.

Status/Duration

The treaty is not in force. Both the United States and Russia ratified START II, but only Russia ratified the 1997 protocol, which extended the deadline for implementation of the treaty. In reaction to the withdrawal of the United States from the Anti-Ballistic Missile Treaty in December 2001, Russia withdrew from the START II treaty in June 2002. Once in force, START II would remain active as long as START I was still in force. At that point, the provisions of both treaties were to be applicable.

Web Resources

For the full text of the treaty and a chronology of events, see the Arms Control Association (www.armscontrol.org/factsheets/start2.asp).

Moscow Treaty (SORT)

Treaty between the United States of America and the Russian Federation on Strategic Offensive Reductions, signed on May 24, 2002, and entered into force on June 1, 2003

Provisions

SORT requires the United States and Russia to reduce the number of deployed strategic nuclear warheads to between 1,700 and 2,200 each by December 31, 2012. The removed warheads do not have to be destroyed; they can be put in storage. Each party is at liberty to determine the composition and structure of its remaining arsenal, and both agree that START I and its provisions remain in force.

Compliance

Through 2009, the verification regime put in place by START I will be used to ensure each party's compliance with the treaty.

Status/Duration

The treaty will remain in force until December 2012. If the parties agree, the treaty can be extended or replaced by another treaty.

Web Resources

For the full text of the treaty and chronology of events, see the United States Department of State (www.state.gov/t/ac/rls/fs/2003/27411.htm).

Chemical Weapons Convention

Convention on the Prohibition of the Development, Production, Stockpiling, and Use of Chemical Weapons and on Their Destruction, opened for signature on January 13, 1993, and entered into force on April 29, 1997

Provisions

States party to the Chemical Weapons Convention vow to refrain from producing, stockpiling, acquiring, transferring, and using chemical weapons. Chemical weapons and chemical weapons production facilities that lie within the jurisdiction of a state party must be destroyed within ten years of the entry into force of the treaty. All chemical weapons stockpiles and facilities and information related to the use and production of chemical weapons must be registered with the Organization for the Prohibition of Chemical Weapons.

Compliance

The Organization for the Prohibition of Chemical Weapons (OPCW) is responsible for monitoring compliance with the treaty, which it does by conducting "routine inspections" of facilities related to the chemical industry that lie within the jurisdiction of the states party to the treaty. If one state party is suspected by another of being in breach of the treaty, the OPCW can conduct a "challenge inspection." However, a challenge inspection can be prevented if at least three-quarters of the OPCW executive body votes against it. If a state party is found to be in noncompliance, the OPCW can recommend that the remaining states enforce collective sanctions. In breaches of "particular gravity," the issue may be brought before the United Nations Security Council, which may decide on additional sanctions.

Status/Duration

As of September 2004, the treaty had been ratified by 164 states. Israel has signed but not ratified the treaty. Notable nonmembers of the treaty are Angola, North Korea, Egypt, Iraq, Lebanon, Somalia, and Syria. Libya ratified the treaty in January 2004. The treaty is of unlimited duration.

Web Resources

For the full text of the treaty and a chronology of events, see the Arms Control Association (www.armscontrol.org/factsheets/cwcglance.asp).

Biological Weapons Convention

Convention on the Prohibition of the Development, Production, and Stockpiling of Bacteriological (Biological) and Toxin Weapons and on Their Destruction, opened for signature on April 10, 1972, and entered into force on March 26, 1975

Provisions

States party to the Biological Weapons Convention vow to refrain from developing, producing, stockpiling, acquiring, or retaining both biological agents or toxins that "have no justification for prophylactic, protective or other peaceful purposes" and "weapons, equipment or means of delivery designed to use such agents or toxins for hostile purposes or in armed conflict." Member states that already have in their possession or under their jurisdiction the type of items referred to must destroy them or divert them to peaceful purposes within nine months after becoming a party to the treaty. Member states are furthermore prohibited from transferring such items to any recipient whatsoever, and they must not encourage or assist any third party wishing to manufacture or acquire them.

Compliance

The treaty does not have a verification regime nor does it specify how its provisions should be enforced. The treaty does suggest that cases of noncompliance can be brought before the United Nations Security Council. In 1994, the Ad Hoc Group was set up to develop a verification regime. In 2001, the group presented a draft verification protocol that was accepted by the majority of member states but rejected by the United States. The United States rejected the protocol because it considered the protocol too weak to verify compliance and believed that the proposed on-site inspection of facilities would endanger both national security and the commercial interests of the United States.

Status/Duration

As of September 2004, the treaty had been ratified by 151 states. The verification protocol is not yet in force. Notable nonmembers are Israel, which has not signed the treaty; and Egypt, Somalia, and Syria, which have signed but not ratified it. The treaty is of unlimited duration. Member states can withdraw from the treaty if doing so is in the supreme interest of their country.

Web Resources

For the full text of the treaty and chronology of events, see the Arms Control Association (www.armscontrol.org/factsheets/bwcataglance. asp).

Geneva Protocol

Protocol for the Prohibition of the Use in War of Asphyxiating, Poisonous, or Other Gases, and of Bacteriological Methods of Warfare, opened for signature on June 17, 1925; enters into force for each state on the date of the deposit of ratification

Provisions

States party to the Geneva Protocol vow to refrain from using asphyxiating, poisonous, or other gases in war as well as bacteriological methods of warfare. The Geneva Protocol does not ban the production, development, or stockpiling of such gases and biological weapons, nor does it apply to internal or civil strife. The United States, China, Israel, Iraq, North Korea, Syria, and Libya have reserved the right to retaliate in kind against a chemical weapons attack.

Compliance

The Geneva Protocol has no verification mechanism; compliance is based on consensual agreement of the contracting parties.

Status/Duration

As of September 2004, the treaty had been ratified by 133 states. The treaty is of unlimited duration.

Web Resources

For the full text of the treaty, see the Monterey Institute for International Studies, Center for Non-Proliferation Studies (cns.miis.edu/pubs/inven/pdfs/aptgenev.pdf).

Outer Space Treaty

Treaty on Principles Governing the Activities of States in the Exploration and Use of Outer Space, Including the Moon and Other Celestial Bodies, opened for signature on January 27, 1967, and entered into force on October 10, 1967

Provisions

States party to the Outer Space Treaty vow to refrain from placing nuclear weapons or other weapons of mass destruction in orbit around the earth and from installing such weapons on the moon or any other celestial body or elsewhere in outer space. The treaty prohibits member states from establishing military bases, installations, or fortifications at the locations referred to and from conducting military maneuvers or testing of any type of weapons at those locations. Although the treaty does not define the meaning of "weapons of mass destruction," the term is generally agreed to include nuclear, chemical, and biological weapons. The treaty emphasizes that space is an international domain open to any country that wishes to explore it for peaceful purposes.

Compliance

The treaty does not have a verification regime. Issues of noncompliance are to be resolved internally among the parties.

Status/Duration

As of September 2004, ninety-eight states had ratified the treaty. The United States, Russia, and China are members of the treaty. One notable nonmember is North Korea, the only nonmember believed to be pursuing space-launch capabilities. The treaty is of unlimited duration. Member states can withdraw if they deem it necessary.

Web Resources

For the full text of the treaty and a summary of its provisions, see the Monterey Institute for International Studies, Center for Non-Proliferation Studies (cns.miis.edu/research/space/treaties).

Convention on Certain Conventional Weapons

Convention on Prohibitions or Restrictions on the Use of Certain Conventional Weapons Which May Be Deemed to Be Excessively Injurious or to Have Indiscriminate Effects, opened for signature on April 10, 1981; entered into force December 2, 1983

Provisions

States party to the Convention on Certain Conventional Weapons vow to refrain from using conventional weapons that create nondetectable fragments when deployed. Mines and booby traps should not be used against civilian populations, nor should booby traps have the appearance of being a harmless object. Member states are furthermore prohibited from using incendiary weapons against civilians and from using air-delivered incendiary devices against military targets located in areas with a high concentration of civilians. Finally, member states are to refrain from using or transferring laser weapons designed to cause permanent blindness. The 1996 amended mine protocol to the Convention on Certain Conventional Weapons places restrictions on the use of antipersonnel mines but does not ban their deployment.

Compliance

The treaty does not have a verification mechanism.

Status/Duration

To become a full party to the treaty, a state has to ratify at least two of the treaty's three original protocols. As of September 2004, ninety-four states had ratified the treaty. Many states that are not party to the Anti-Personnel Land Mine Treaty (Ottawa Convention)—most notably the United States, China, India, Israel, Pakistan, and Russia—are members of the Convention on Certain Conventional Weapons.

Web Resources

For the full text of the treaty and all the protocols as well as a chronology of events, see United Nations Department of Disarmament (//disarmament2.un.org/ccw/).

Anti-Personnel Land Mine Treaty

1997 Convention on the Prohibition of the Use, Stockpiling, Production, and Transfer of Anti-Personnel Mines and on Their Destruction, opened for signature on December 3, 1997, and entered into force on March 1, 1999

Provisions

States party to the Anti-Personnel Land Mine Treaty (Ottawa Convention) vow to refrain from using, developing, acquiring, retaining, stockpiling, or transferring antipersonnel land mines. The treaty defines antipersonnel land mines as mines "designed to be exploded by the presence, proximity, or contact of a person and that will incapacitate, injure or kill one or more persons"; this definition excludes explosive devices such as claymores and antivehicle mines that are triggered by remote control. States should destroy all stockpiles of antipersonnel mines in their arsenals within four years of becoming a party to the treaty. Limited quantities of mines are allowed to be retained for training purposes. In addition to destroying all antipersonnel land mines in their arsenals, member states must eradicate all antipersonnel land mines that have been deployed within their territorial borders or jurisdiction within ten years of becoming a party to the treaty. The treaty urges states that are in a position to do so to assist other states in their de-mining and destruction efforts.

Compliance

The treaty does not have a verification mechanism. Parties are required to report to the United Nations the number, type, and location of their antipersonnel land mines and how much progress is being made in destroying them. If a member state is suspected to be in breach of the treaty, a fact-finding team can be sent to investigate.

Status/Duration

As of September 2004, 143 states had ratified the treaty. Notable nonmember states are the United States, Russia, China, India, Pakistan, and a majority of the states in the Middle East. The treaty is of unlimited duration.

Web Resources

For the full text of the treaty and a chronology of events, see the Human Rights Watch (www.hrw.org/doc/?t=arms_landmines).

Treaty on Conventional Armed Forces in Europe

Opened for signature on November 19, 1990, and entered into force on November 9, 1992

Provisions

The Treaty on Conventional Armed Forces in Europe (the CFE treaty) calls for reductions of major armaments (battle tanks, armored combat vehicles, artillery pieces, combat aircraft, and attack helicopters) to equal levels stipulated for members of NATO and of the Warsaw Pact. The treaty's area of application includes the "entire land territory of the States Parties in Europe from the Atlantic Ocean to the Ural Mountains, including all the European island territories of the States Parties." Subzone areas of application are located at the far north and south and are subject to specific flank limits. States party to the treaty must inform each other of their armament levels. If a state party wishes to increase its holdings to a level exceeding the level set forth by the treaty, it must give the other states ninety days' notice before doing so. Nevertheless, such increases are not to exceed the limit for the overall aggregate level of armament allowed under either NATO or the Warsaw Pact. The reduction of arms was to be implemented in three phases and completed no more than forty months after the treaty entered into force. States' excess armaments can be either destroyed, converted to nonmilitary uses, placed on public display, used as ground targets, or decommissioned. States party to the treaty must inform each other of the location of storage facilities and destruction sites for armaments covered by the treaty. The reduction process is subject to compulsory on-site inspections.

On July 10, 1992, the contracting parties of the CFE treaty signed the Concluding Act of the Negotiation on Personnel Strength of Conventional Armed Forces in Europe (CFE 1-A Agreement), a politically binding agreement that came into force on November 19, 1992. It sets limits on levels of all military personnel except naval forces, internal security forces, and forces under United Nations command. National personnel limits can be changed if the parties give prior notification of their intent to do so. If the change involves an increase in personnel, the party must give the other parties the reasons why an increase is warranted. If states wish to react to such notification, they may call an extraordinary conference.

Compliance

The Joint Consultative Group is in charge of verification. States party to the convention have to accept inspections by other states, but they also are entitled to carry out inspections themselves. The parties are furthermore entitled to use national or multinational technical means to verify compliance. Using concealment measures in an effort to obstruct verification is forbidden.

Status/Duration

Because of the disintegration of the Soviet Union, the treaty was revised, and the Agreement on the Adaptation of the CFE Treaty was signed on November 19, 1999. Instead of block limitations, the adapted treaty was to set national and territorial ceilings on conventional armaments and equipment. States party to the treaty were to be allowed to temporarily exceed the limits set forth by the treaty during short-term deployments and military exercises. National and territorial limits were to be equal, except when arms are deployed in support of a mission of the United Nations or the Organization for Security and Cooperation in Europe. The adapted CFE treaty will enter into force when all thirty member states have ratified the treaty. The United States and eighteen other states have declared that they will not ratify the adapted CFE treaty until Russia fulfills its commitments according to the Concluding Act of the Negotiation on Personnel Strength of Conventional Armed Forces in Europe (CFE 1-A Agreement). Because Russia has been unwilling to withdraw weapons regulated by the treaty from Georgia and Moldova, the adapted CFE treaty has yet to come into effect. As a consequence, the provisions of the original CFE treaty are still in force.

Web Resources

For the full text of the treaty and a chronology of events, see the Arms Control Association (www.armscontrol.org/factsheets/).

Treaty on Open Skies

Opened for signature on March 24, 1992, and entered into force on January 1, 2002

Provisions

States party to the Treaty on Open Skies have the right to conduct unarmed observation flights over each other's territory to ensure the transparency of military activities. Each member state must accept a "passive quota" of flights sent out to observe its territory, and each has an "active quota" of flights that it can send out to monitor other members' territories. A state wishing to conduct observation flights over another state's territory must give that state seventy-two hours' advance notice. The monitoring state must supply the information gathered from an observation flight to the state that was observed, and the monitoring state must furthermore provide all other member states with a mission report and allow them to purchase the data obtained.

Compliance

The Open Skies Consultative Commission is in charge of verification.

Status/Duration

As of September 2004, thirty states had ratified the treaty. The treaty is of unlimited duration.

Web Resources

For the full text of the treaty and a summary of its provisions, see the Arms Control Association (www.armscontrol.org/factsheets/openskies.asp?print).

Australia Group

Established in 1985

Provisions

The group is a voluntary association whose goal is to prevent the proliferation of chemical and biological weapons by enforcing provisions of national export laws concerning chemical precursors, chemical and biological weapons equipment, and biological weapons, organisms, and agents. All members of the Australia Group must be party to the Chemical Weapons Convention and the Biological Weapons Convention.

Member states must require licenses for the following material and items:

—dual-use chemical manufacturing facilities, equipment, and related technology

—plant pathogens

—animal pathogens

—biological agents

—dual-use biological equipment.

Member states must keep control lists of the following agents:

—chemical weapons precursors

—dual-use chemical manufacturing facilities, equipment, and related technology

—plant pathogens

—animal pathogens

—biological agents

—dual-use biological equipment.

Exports of such materials should be denied if there are concerns that the material could be diverted to produce chemical and biological weapons. The material and agents covered by the Australia Group are continually reviewed and modified to reflect the changing international security environment and scientific developments.

Status

As of September 2004, the group had thirty-eight members. Notable nonmembers include Israel, Iran, North Korea, and Syria. The United States is a member.

Web Resources

For more on the group and its export provisions, see the Australia Group (www.australiagroup.net/index_en.htm).

Nuclear Suppliers Group

Established in 1975

Provisions

Members of the Nuclear Suppliers Group (NSG), a voluntary association of nuclear supplier states, aim to promote the nonproliferation of nuclear weapons and nuclear explosive devices by enforcing strict control of the export of civilian nuclear material, nuclear-related material, and nuclear technology to all non-nuclear states. By doing so they aim to prevent nuclear material intended for civilian purposes from being used to develop nuclear weapons. NSG guidelines fall into two categories. The first category includes nuclear material, nuclear reactors and equipment, and equipment devoted to nuclear enrichment and reprocessing. The second category includes items and technologies that can be used for both civilian purposes and production of nuclear weapons. In 1994, the NSG adopted a "nonproliferation principle" that states that a supplier should authorize the transfer of nuclear-related material only when it is confident that the material will not be used to develop weapons.

States importing nuclear-related material must show that they have enforced sufficient physical security measures to safeguard the material and vow not to transfer the imported material to a third party. Before a transfer of nuclear material, nuclear reactors and equipment, or equipment devoted to nuclear enrichment and reprocessing can be approved, importing states must agree to establish IAEA safeguards in all their nuclear activities and facilities. Before a transfer of dual-use items and technologies can be approved, they must enforce IAEA safeguards for the specific nuclear activity or facility involved in the transfer.

Compliance

The IAEA is in charge of verifying that non–nuclear weapons states wishing to engage in trade of nuclear-related material with members of the group do not intend to use the material to produce nuclear weapons. The NSG has no legal enforcement mechanism to ensure compliance with the additional restrictions it places on its members' activities.

Status

As of September 2004, the group had forty members. To become a member, a state must be in compliance with the Nuclear Non-

Proliferation Treaty or a regional nuclear nonproliferation agreement. The United States is a member of the group. Notable nonmembers are India, Israel, Pakistan, and North Korea. China applied to join the NSG in January 2004.

Web Resources

For more on the group and its export provisions, see the Nuclear Suppliers Group (www.nuclearsuppliersgroup.org/).

Zangger Committee

Established in 1971

Provisions

Members of the Zangger Committee (ZAC), a voluntary association, vow not to transfer specific nuclear-related materials that can be used to develop nuclear weapons to states that are not party to the Nuclear Non-Proliferation Treaty (NPT) unless those states have enforced IAEA safeguards. The controlled items are included on the Trigger List, which has been amended several times by committee members.

Compliance

ZAC has no legal enforcement mechanism to ensure compliance.

Status

As of September 2004, ZAC had twenty-four members. ZAC's mission was largely taken over by the Nuclear Suppliers Group when the group was created in 1975. Not only did the NSG incorporate the Trigger List in its provisions on controlling exports of nuclear-related material, it also applied its export controls to all non-nuclear states, not only to non-members of the NPT.

Web Resources

For more on the group and its export provisions, see the Zangger Committee (www.zanggercommittee.org).

Wassenaar Arrangement

Wassenaar Arrangement on Export Controls for Conventional Arms and Dual-Use Goods and Technologies, established in 1996

Provisions

Members of the Wassenaar Arrangement, a voluntary group, aim to control the export of especially sensitive and dangerous dual-use goods and technologies and conventional arms and to promote the mutual exchange of information about such exports. By complementing and reinforcing the provisions on national export control systems set up by the former Coordinating Committee for Multilateral Export Controls (COCOM) and existing control regimes, the Wassenaar Arrangement seeks to ensure that transfer or diversion of items referred to in the agreement do not enhance a state's military capabilities in such a way that deployment of the items would destabilize the international security environment. Unlike COCOM, the agreement does not give members the right to veto another state's decision to transfer such items. Conventional weapons referred to in the agreement include battle tanks, armored combat vehicles, large-caliber artillery, military aircraft/ unmanned aerial vehicles, military and attack helicopters, warships, and missiles and missile systems. The agreement classifies stealth technology and advanced radar as "very sensitive" items, and members are to "exert extreme vigilance" when exporting them. In 2000, parties to the agreement recognized the need to impose export controls on Man-Portable Air Defense Systems (MANPADS).

Compliance

The agreement has no legal enforcement mechanism to ensure compliance. Nevertheless, in December 2000, member states agreed on a set of "non-binding best practices" meant to ensure effective enforcement of the provisions on disposal of surplus military equipment, of export controls on very sensitive items, and of national export controls in general. In December 2002, members agreed to another set of "best practices," on the export of small arms and light weapons.

Status/Duration

As of June 2004, the agreement had thirty-three members, including the United States. Notable nonmembers include Belarus, China, Israel, and South Africa, all of which are major arms exporters.

Web Resources

For more on the committee and its provisions, see the Wassenaar Arrangement (www.wassenaar.org/).

Missile Technology Control Regime

Established in 1987

Provisions

States that are members of the Missile Technology Control Regime (MTCR), a voluntary group, put in place national controls to restrict the export of missile delivery systems that could be used for a nuclear, biological, or chemical attack. They do not regulate manned aircraft or national space programs. Members should control the transfer of two categories of items: Category I material includes complete rocket and unmanned aerial vehicle delivery systems and subsystems; Category II material includes propulsion and propellant components and launch and ground support equipment and material for its construction. Transfer of Category I material is strictly forbidden; transfer of Category II material, although less forcefully forbidden, still warrants end-use certification or verification. The regime covers missiles capable of delivering a payload of at least 500 kilograms a distance of 300 kilometers or more. Ballistic missiles, space launch vehicles, and sounding rockets are considered to be missiles. Unmanned aerial vehicles include cruise missiles, remotely piloted vehicles, and drones.

When deciding whether to export the items referred to above, member states should evaluate

—whether the importer has ambitions to acquire weapons of mass destruction

—the purposes and capabilities of the importer's space and missile programs

—what consequences exporting the item will have on the importer's ability to develop a system to deliver weapons of mass destruction

—whether the importer's stated use for the item is credible

—whether a transfer would breach any multilateral treaty.

In November 2002, MTCR members initiated the International Code of Conduct against Ballistic Missile Proliferation. The initiative calls on all countries to refrain from producing more ballistic missiles capable of carrying weapons of mass destruction and to reduce their current arsenals of such missiles. Countries participating in the initiative exchange information on their space launch and ballistic missile programs and give each other prior notice of their ballistic missile launches or launches of space launch vehicles.

Compliance

The MTCR has no legal enforcement mechanism to ensure compliance. U.S. law, however, imposes sanctions on any state, company, or individual that exports items covered by the MTCR.

Status

The control regime has thirty-four members, including the United States. Israel, Romania, and the Slovak Republic have vowed to abide by the MTCR's rules although they are not party to the treaty. Notable nonmembers include India, Iran, Pakistan, Syria, and North Korea. All MTCR countries, with the exception of Brazil, have adopted the International Code of Conduct against Ballistic Missile Proliferation. In all, more than 100 states have signed up to participate in the MTCR initiative to adopt the code of conduct.

Web Resources

For more on the committee and its provisions, see the Missile Technology Control Regime (www.mtcr.info/english/index.html).

United States–North Korea Agreed Framework

Agreed Framework between the United States of America and the Democratic People's Republic of Korea, opened for signature on October 21, 1994; no longer in force as of January 10, 2003

Provisions

The United States–North Korea Agreed Framework aimed to end North Korea's nuclear weapons program and the development of nuclear-related infrastructure causing high proliferation concerns in exchange for U.S. nuclear energy, economic, and diplomatic reimbursements. As a party to the framework North Korea was obliged to

—freeze and then dismantle its graphite-moderated experimental research reactor; seal, cease activities at, and dismantle reprocessing facilities; find a safe way to store the spent fuel from its experimental reactor and dispose of the fuel in a safe fashion without reprocessing it in North Korea; and dismantle its two larger, partially constructed power reactors.

—give full access to International Atomic Energy Association (IAEA) to monitor the freeze on its reactors; allow implementation of IAEA safety guidelines as required of states that are party to the Nuclear Non-Proliferation Treaty (NPT) as well as allow IAEA inspectors to resume ad hoc and routine inspections of facilities not subject to the freeze until the supply agreement for the light water reactor (LWR) project has been concluded; and continue to be a party to the NPT.

—work to implement the Joint Declaration of South and North Korea on the Denuclearization of the Korean Peninsula as well as engage in dialogue with South Korea.

The United States was in turn to provide North Korea with

—Two light water reactors (LWRs) with a generating capacity of approximately 2,000 megawatts to be financed and provided by an international consortium, by 2003.

—150,000 tons of heavy fuel oil for heating and electricity production to replace energy that North Korea would have produced if not for the freeze on its graphite-moderated reactors, by October 1995. Afterward, 500,000 tons of oil was be provided annually until the first LWR was completed.

—Formal assurance that it would not use or threaten to use nuclear weapons against North Korea.

Furthermore, both countries were to work to

—reduce barriers to trade and investment

—open liaison offices in Washington and Pyongyang

—upgrade bilateral relations to the ambassadorial level as issues of concern to both parties were resolved.

Compliance

The body responsible for monitoring verification of the Agreed Framework was the Korean Peninsula Energy Development Organization (KEDO). In case of noncompliance, the issue was to be deferred to the IAEA.

Status

The Agreed Framework is no longer in force. On October 16, 2002, North Korean officials reportedly admitted that they had a uranium-enrichment program, thereby confirming American suspicions that the country was covertly trying to develop another nuclear weapons program and hence was in breach of the framework. On January 10, 2003, North Korea announced that it was withdrawing from the Nuclear Non-Proliferation Treaty and expelled IAEA inspectors. On February 5, 2003, Pyongyang announced that the five-megawatt Yongbyon nuclear reactor had been reactivated. Plutonium at Yongbyon was also repossessed.

Web Resources

For the full text of the agreement, see the United States Department of State (www.state.gov/t/ac/rls/or/2004/31009.htm).

Notes

Chapter One

1. For related views, see Ronald F. Lehman II, "Arms Control: Passing the Torch as Time Runs Out," *Washington Quarterly* (Summer 1993): 37–52; Avis Bohlen, "The Rise and Fall of Arms Control," *Survival* 45, no. 3 (Autumn 2003): 7–34; and Michael O. Wheeler, "The American Approach to Arms Control," in *Perspectives on Arms Control*, edited by Michael O. Wheeler, James M. Smith, and Glenn M. Segell, INS Occasional Paper 55 (U.S. Air Force Academy: Institute for National Security Studies, 2004), pp. 1–52. See also Paul Bracken, "Thinking (Again) about Arms Control," *Orbis* (Winter 2004).

2. George Perkovich and others, "Universal Compliance: A Strategy for Nuclear Security," Carnegie Endowment for International Peace, June 2004, p. 11.

3. See for example, McGeorge Bundy, *Danger and Survival* (New York: Vintage Books, 1988), pp. 574–617; and Frank von Hippel, *Citizen Scientist* (New York: Touchstone Books, 1991), pp. 99–104.

4. According to Soviet ambassador Anatoly Dobrynin, "[T]he increased defense spending provoked by Reagan's policies was not the straw that broke the back of the evil empire. We did not bankrupt ourselves in the arms race as the Caspar Weinbergers of this world would like to believe. The Soviet response to Star Wars caused only an acceptable small rise in defense spending. Throughout the Reagan Presidency the rising Soviet defense effort contributed to our economic decline, but only marginally as it had in previous years. . . . It may sound like a historical paradox . . . but if the President had not abandoned his hostile stance toward the Soviet Union for a more constructive one during his second

term, Gorbachev would not have been able to launch his reforms and his new thinking. Quite the contrary, Gorbachev would have been forced to continue the conservative foreign and defense policies of his predecessors in defense of the nation against America." See Anatoly Dobrynin, quoted in William D. Jackson, "Soviet Reassessment of Ronald Reagan, 1985–1988," *Political Science Quarterly* (Winter 1998–99): 643–44.

5. Raymond L. Garthoff, *Détente and Confrontation: American-Soviet Relations from Nixon to Reagan*, rev. ed. (Brookings, 1994), pp. 27–73.

6. Clifford Gaddy and Fiona Hill, *Putin's Agenda, America's Choice: Russia's Search for Strategic Stability*, Brookings Policy Brief 99 (May 2002); for a story of how the relationship evolved in the early to mid-1990s, see also Ashton B. Carter and William J. Perry, *Preventive Defense: A New Security Strategy for America* (Brookings, 1999), pp. 8–91.

7. "START II and Its Extension Protocol at a Glance," Arms Control Association fact sheet, May 14, 2004 (available at www.armscontrol.org/factsheets/start2.asp).

8. James M. Lindsay and Michael O'Hanlon, *Defending America: The Case for Limited National Missile Defense* (Brookings, 2001), p. 17.

9. For the likely costs of a war to overthrow the North Korean regime, for example—traditionally estimated in the many hundreds of thousands of lives and even under more optimistic assumptions surely in the many tens of thousands—see Michael O'Hanlon and Mike Mochizuki, *Crisis on the Korean Peninsula* (New York: McGraw-Hill, 2003): 60–62.

10. For a good articulation of this, see "Expounding Bush's Approach to U.S. Nuclear Security: An Interview with John R. Bolton," *Arms Control Today* 32 (March 2002): p. 8.

11. For intriguing ideas with a great deal of merit, yet ones that could constrain American power too much for the good of the international system if pursued too quickly, see Paul B. Stares and John D. Steinbruner, "Cooperative Security in the New Europe," in *The New Germany and the New Europe*, edited by Paul B. Stares (Brookings, 1992), pp. 218–48; and Janne E. Nolan, ed., *Global Engagement: Cooperation and Security in the 21st Century* (Brookings, 1994). For a more recent summary of the cooperative security concept, see Stanley Foundation, "Global Disarmament Regimes: A Future or a Failure?" (2003), available at www.reports.stanleyfoundation.org.

12. This is not a new insight. See, for example, T. Schelling and M. Halperin, *Strategy and Arms Control* (New York: Twentieth Century Fund, 1961).

13. For much of the richness of this debate over recent decades, see Hedley Bull, *The Anarchical Society: A Study of Order in World Politics* (Columbia University Press, 1977); Richard Falk, "What New System of World Order?" in *Toward a Just World Order*, edited by Richard Falk, Samuel S. Kim, and Saul H. Mendlovitz (Boulder, Colo.: Westview, 1982), pp. 537–58; Ernst B. Haas, *Beyond*

the Nation-State (Stanford University Press, 1964); John J. Mearsheimer, *The Tragedy of Great Power Politics* (New York: W. W. Norton, 2001); and Richard H. Ullman, *Securing Europe* (Princeton University Press, 1991).

14. Joseph S. Nye, *The Paradox of American Power: Why the World's Only Superpower Can't Go It Alone* (Oxford University Press, 2002).

15. Nye, *The Paradox of American Power*, pp. 159–63.

16. See for example, Robert Gilpin, *War and Change in World Politics* (Cambridge University Press, 1981); and Kenneth N. Waltz, *Theory of International Politics* (New York: Random House, 1979).

17. See Stephen M. Walt, "Alliance Formation and the Balance of World Power," *International Security*, vol. 9 (Spring 1985), reprinted in Michael E. Brown, Sean M. Lynn-Jones, and Steven E. Miller, eds., *The Perils of Anarchy: Contemporary Realism and International Security* (MIT Press, 1995), pp. 208–48.

18. Thomas C. Schelling, "Foreword," in *Arms Control: Cooperative Security in a Changing Environment*, edited by Jeffrey A. Larsen (Boulder, Colo.: Lynne Rienner Publishers, 2002), p. xiv.

19. Matthew Bunn, Anthony Wier, and John P. Holdren, *Controlling Nuclear Warheads and Materials: A Report Card and Action Plan* (Washington: NTI and Harvard University), March 2003.

20. U.S. Congress, Office of Technology Assessment, *Proliferation of Weapons of Mass Destruction: Assessing the Risks* (Government Printing Office, 1983).

21. Ibid.

22. Michael A. Levi and Henry C. Kelly, "Weapons of Mass Disruption," *Scientific American*, December 2002; Peter D. Zimmerman, "Dirty Bombs: The Threat Revisited," *Defense Horizons* 38 (January 2004), Center for Technology and National Security, National Defense University.

23. Albert Wohlstetter and others, "Swords from Plowshares: The Military Potential of Civilian Nuclear Energy" (University of Chicago Press, 1979).

24. John J. Mearsheimer, "Back to the Future: Instability in Europe after the Cold War," *International Security* 15 (Summer 1990); Kenneth N. Waltz, "More May Be Better," in *The Spread of Nuclear Weapons: A Debate*, by Kenneth N. Waltz and Scott D. Sagan (New York: W. W. Norton), 1995.

25. For example, Scott D. Sagan, *The Limits of Safety: Organizations, Accidents, and Nuclear Weapons* (Princeton University Press), 1993; and Bruce G. Blair, *The Logic of Accidental Nuclear War* (Brookings, 1993).

26. Joseph S. Nye Jr., "Maintaining a Nonproliferation Regime," *International Organization* (Winter 1981).

27. Ibid.

28. For a view that similarly emphasizes the right of the international community to take coercive action against proliferators but constrains the range of enforcement actions more narrowly than we do, see Perkovich and others, *Universal Compliance*, p. 15.

29. Ann Devroy, "Pact Reached to Dismantle Ukraine's Nuclear Force," *Washington Post*, January 10, 1994, p. A1; Letter from the Permanent Representatives of the Russian Federation, Ukraine, the United Kingdom, and the United States to the United Nations, December 19, 1994, document A/49/765 and S/1994/1399.

30. Schelling and Halperin, *Strategy and Arms Control*, p. 2.

31. See Ivo Daalder, *Cooperative Arms Control: A New Agenda for the Post-Cold War Era*, CISSM Paper 1 (College Park, Md.: Center for International Security Studies at Maryland School of Public Affairs, October 1992).

Chapter Two

1. Rose Gottemoeller, *Beyond Arms Control: How to Deal with Nuclear Weapons*, Policy Brief 23 (Washington: Carnegie Endowment for International Peace), February 2003.

2. For explanations of some of the reasons that people were worried about withdrawal from the ABM Treaty, see Joseph Cirincione and Jon B. Wolfsthal, "What If the New Strategic Framework Goes Bad?" *Arms Control Today* 31 (November 2001): 6–12; Senator Carl Levin, "A Debate Deferred: Missile Defense after the September 11 Attacks," *Arms Control Today* 31 (November 2001): 3–5; and James M. Lindsay and Michael E. O'Hanlon, *Defending America: The Case for Limited National Missile Defense* (Brookings, 2001), pp. 116–47.

3. See Celeste A. Wallander, "Russia's Strategic Priorities," *Arms Control Today* 32 (January/February 2002): 4–6; Bates Gill, "Can China's Tolerance Last?" *Arms Control Today* 32 (January/February 2002): 7–9; and Joanne Tompkins, "How U.S. Strategic Policy Is Changing China's Nuclear Plans," *Arms Control Today* 33 (January/February 2003): 11–15.

4. "Letter of Transmittal and Article-by-Article Analysis of the Treaty on Strategic Offensive Reductions," *Arms Control Today* 32 (July/August 2002): 28–30.

5. "Russia's National Security Document," *Arms Control Today* 30 (January/February 2000): 15–20.

6. See Roger Molander, David Mosher, and Lowell Schwartz, *Nuclear Weapons and the Future of Strategic Warfare* (Santa Monica, Calif.: RAND, 2002), pp. xiv-xxvi.

7. Desmond Ball, "The Development of the SIOP, 1960–1983," in *Strategic Nuclear Targeting*, edited by Desmond Ball and Jeffrey Richelson (Cornell University Press, 1986), pp. 66–70; McGeorge Bundy, *Danger and Survival* (New York: Vintage Books, 1988); Harold A. Feiveson, ed., *The Nuclear Turning Point* (Brookings, 1999); and David Mosher and Michael O'Hanlon, *The START Treaty and Beyond* (Washington: Congressional Budget Office, 1991), pp. 14–15.

For a similar argument about offensive forces, see Jan Lodal, *The Price of Dominance* (New York: Council on Foreign Relations, 2001), pp. 84–87.

8. See Brad Roberts, "Tripolar Stability: The Future of Nuclear Relations among the United States, Russia, and China," IDA Paper P-3727 (September 2002), pp. S-1 through S-8.

9. Andrew M. Sessler and others, *Countermeasures* (Cambridge, Mass.: Union of Concerned Scientists), 2000.

10. Michael Levi, "A Nuclear Option That America Does Not Need," *Financial Times* (London), August 15, 2003.

11. C. Paul Robinson, *Pursuing a New Nuclear Weapons Policy for the 21st Century* (Sandia, N.M.: Sandia National Laboratory, 2001).

12. Robert W. Nelson, "Low-Yield Earth-Penetrating Nuclear Weapons," *Science and Global Security* 10, no. 1 (2002).

13. Michael A. Levi, "Dreaming of Clean Nukes," *Nature* 428 (April 29, 2004), p. 892.

14. See, for example, Robert C. Aldridge, *Precision Guided Munitions and the Neutron Bomb* (Washington: Cato Institute, 1982).

15. Michael M. May and Zachary Haldeman, *Effectiveness of Nuclear Weapons against Buried Biological Agents* (Stanford University, 2003).

16. Michael A. Levi, *Fire in the Hole: Nuclear and Non-Nuclear Options for Counterproliferation* (Washington: Carnegie Endowment for International Peace, 2002).

17. Terry L. Deibel, "The Death of a Treaty," *Foreign Affairs* 81, no. 5 (September/October 2002).

18. Helen Dewar, "Senate Rejects Test Ban Treaty; Nuclear Pact Falls 51 to 48 as GOP Deals Clinton Major Defeat," *Washington Post*, October 14, 1999, p. A1.

19. Governor George W. Bush and Vice President Al Gore, "Presidential Election Forum: The Candidates on Arms Control," *Arms Control Today* 30 (September 2000): 3–7.

20. *Technical Issues Related to Ratification of the Comprehensive Test Ban Treaty* (Washington: National Academy of Sciences Press, 2002).

21. Richard L. Garwin, in testimony before the U.S. Senate Committee on Foreign Relations, *The Comprehensive Test Ban Treaty*, October 7, 1999.

22. Stephen M. Younger, "Nuclear Weapons in the Twenty-First Century," LAUR-00-2850 (Los Alamos, N.M.: Los Alamos National Laboratory, 2000).

23. *Technical Issues Related to Ratification of the Comprehensive Test Ban Treaty* (Washington: National Academy of Sciences Press, 2002).

24. Ibid.

25. See, for example, Bruce G. Blair, *Global Zero Alert for Nuclear Forces* (Brookings, 1995).

26. David E. Mosher and others, *Beyond the Nuclear Shadow: A Phased Approach for Improving Nuclear Safety and U.S.-Russian Relations* (Santa Monica, Calif.: RAND, 2003).

27. See, for example, Robert Joseph and Ronald Lehman, eds., *U.S. Nuclear Policy in the 21st Century* (Government Printing Office, 1998).

28. Ibid.

29. Center for Security Policy, "Unilateral Nuclear Disarmament by Any Other Name Is Still Recklessly Irresponsible; Will Clinton Be Allowed to Do It?" January 13, 1998 (www.centerforsecuritypolicy.org/index.jsp?section=papers&code=98-D_06 [September 2, 2004]).

30. O'Hanlon and Lindsay, *Defending America.*

31. See, for example, Feiveson, ed., *The Nuclear Turning Point*; and Mosher and others, *Beyond the Nuclear Shadow.*

32. Feiveson, ed., *The Nuclear Turning Point.*

33. Mosher and others, *Beyond the Nuclear Shadow.*

34. This section draws heavily on Michael O'Hanlon, *Neither Sanctuary nor Star Wars* (Brookings, 2004).

35. See, for example, Theresa Hitchens, "Monsters and Shadows: Left Unchecked, American Fears Regarding Threats to Space Assets Will Drive Weaponization," *Disarmament Forum* 1 (2003), p. 24.

36. See Transcript of the Panel Discussion Held in the United Nations on October 19, 2000 by the NGO Committee on Disarmament (www.igc.org/disarm/T191000outerspace.htm [September 8, 2004]); and Statement by Mr. Hu Xiaodi, Ambassador for Disarmament Affairs of China, at the Plenary of the Conference on Disarmament, June 7, 2001 (www3.itu.int/missions/China/disarmament/2001files/disarmdoc010607.htm; and "China, Russia Want Space Weapons Banned," *Philadelphia Inquirer*, August 23, 2002.

37. See Canada: Working Paper Concerning CD Action on Outer Space, January 21, 1998 (www.unog.ch/disarm/curdoc/1487.htm [September 8, 2004]); James Clay Moltz, "Breaking the Deadlock on Space Arms Control," *Arms Control Today* (April 2002), available at www.armscontrol.org/act/2002_04/moltzapril02.asp?print (September 2, 2004).

38. Peter L. Hays, *United States Military Space: Into the Twenty-First Century* (Montgomery, Ala.: Air University Press, 2002), pp. 11–13; Alvin and Heidi Toffler, *War and Anti-War: Survival at the Dawn of the 21st Century* (Boston: Little, Brown, 1993); Stuart E. Johnson and Martin C. Libicki, eds., *Dominant Battlespace Knowledge* (Washington: National Defense University Press, 1996); Thomas A. Keaney and Eliot A. Cohen, *Gulf War Air Power Survey Summary Report* (Government Printing Office, 1993); William Owens, *Lifting the Fog of War* (New York: Farrar, Straus, and Giroux, 2000); Daniel Goure and Christopher M. Szara, eds., *Air and Space Power in the New Millennium* (Washington: Center for Strategic and International Studies, 1997); Defense Science Board 1996

Summer Study Task Force, *Tactics and Technology for 21st Century Military Superiority* (Department of Defense, 1996); Harlan Ullman and others, *Shock and Awe: Achieving Rapid Dominance* (Washington: National Defense University Press, 1996); George and Meredith Friedman, *The Future of War: Power, Technology, and American World Dominance in the 21st Century* (New York: Crown Publishers, 1996); John Arquilla and David Ronfeldt, eds., *In Athena's Camp: Preparing for Conflict in the Information Age* (Santa Monica, Calif.: RAND, 1997); National Defense Panel, *Transforming Defense: National Security in the 21st Century* (Arlington, Va.: December 1997); and Joint Chiefs of Staff, *Joint Vision 2010* and *Joint Vision 2020* (Department of Defense).

39. Barry Watts, *The Military Uses of Space: A Diagnostic Assessment*, report, Center for Strategic and Budgetary Assessments, February 2001, pp. 29–30.

40. See Paul B. Stares, *Space and National Security* (Brookings, 1987), p. 147.

41. Peter L. Hays, "Military Space Cooperation: Opportunities and Challenges," in *Future Security in Space: Commercial, Military, and Arms Control Trade-Offs*, edited by James Clay Moltz, Occasional Paper 10 (Monterey, Calif.: Monterey Institute of International Studies, 2002), p. 37.

42. This view is hardly confined to conservatives; see for example, Ashton Carter, "Satellites and Anti-Satellites: The Limits of the Possible," *International Security* 10 (Spring 1986): 47.

43. Jonathan Dean, "Defenses in Space: Treaty Issues," in *Future Security in Space*, edited by Moltz, p. 4.

44. Donald Rumsfeld, chairman, *Report of the Commission to Assess United States National Security Space Management and Organization* (U.S. Congress, January 2001).

45. Secretary of Defense Donald H. Rumsfeld, *Quadrennial Defense Review Report 2001* (Department of Defense, 2001), p. 45.

46. Benjamin S. Lambeth, *Mastering the Ultimate High Ground* (Santa Monica, Calif.: RAND, 2003), p. 88.

47. Michael Krepon with Christopher Clary, *Space Assurance or Space Dominance? The Case against Weaponizing Space* (Washington: Henry L. Stimson Center, 2003), p. 21; and Marc Lallanilla, "Shooting Stars: U.S. Military Takes First Step towards Weapons in Space," March 30, 2004 (abcnews.com).

48. See Rebecca Johnson, *Missile Defence and the Weaponisation of Space*, ISIS Policy Paper on Ballistic Missile Defence 11 (London: International Security Information Service, January 2003), available at www.isisuk.demon.co.uk; Dean, "Defenses in Space: Treaty Issues," p. 4; George Bunn and John B. Rhinelander, "Outer Space Treaty May Ban Strike Weapons," *Arms Control Today* 32 (June 2002): 24; and Lt. Col. Bruce M. Deblois, "Space Sanctuary: A Viable National Strategy," *Aerospace Power Journal* (Winter 1998), p. 41.

49. For a proposal along these lines, see Krepon with Clary, *Space Assurance or Space Dominance?* pp. 109–110.

50. For an earlier, highly sophisticated argument along these lines, see John Tirman, ed., *The Fallacy of Star Wars* (New York: Vintage Books, 1984).

51. See O'Hanlon, *Neither Sanctuary nor Star Wars.*

52. For a good discussion, see Krepon with Clary, *Space Assurance or Space Dominance?* pp. 114–24.

53. For an example of a specific proposal along these times, see Michael Krepon, "Model Code of Conduct for the Prevention of Incidents and Dangerous Military Practices in Outer Space" (Washington: Henry L. Stimson Center, 2004).

54. Krepon with Clary, *Space Assurance or Space Dominance?* p. 93.

55. For a summary, see Mosher and O'Hanlon, *The START Treaty and Beyond*, pp. 34–35; Ivo H. Daalder, *Cooperative Arms Control: A New Agenda for the Post-Cold War Era*, CISSM Paper 1, University of Maryland, College Park (October 1992), pp. 23–27.

56. Hays, "Military Space Cooperation: Opportunities and Challenges," in *Future Security in Space*, edited by Moltz, p. 42.

Chapter Three

1. See, for example, Wolfgang K. H. Panofsky, "Dismantling the Concept of 'Weapons of Mass Destruction,'" *Arms Control Today* 28 (April 1998).

2. For defense against ballistic missiles, see, for example, Michael E. O'Hanlon and James M. Lindsay, *Defending America: The Case for Limited National Missile Defense* (Brookings, 2001); for defense against smuggled weapons, see, for example, Michael M. May, Tonya L. Putnam, and Dean Wilkening, *Container Security Report* (Stanford University, 2002).

3. For an introduction to possible consequence mitigation measures, see Lynn E. Davis and others, *Individual Preparedness and Response to Chemical, Radiological, Nuclear, and Biological Terrorist Attacks* (Santa Monica, Calif.: RAND, 2003).

4. For another comprehensive strategy for preventing nuclear terrorism, which contains some elements in common with the strategy developed here as well as other approaches, see Graham Allison, *Nuclear Terrorism* (New York: Times Books, 2004).

5. For a short history of these programs, see Kenneth N. Luongo and William E. Hoehn III, "Reform and Expansion of Threat Reduction," *Arms Control Today* 33 (June 2003).

6. *The Nunn-Lugar Vision: 1992–2002* (Washington: Nuclear Threat Initiative, 2003).

7. Matthew Bunn, John P. Holdren, and Anthony Weir, *Controlling Nuclear Warheads and Materials: A Report Card and Action Plan* (Harvard University, 2003).

8. Daniel Schack, "Congress Approves $79 Billion Supplemental War Budget," *Arms Control Today* 33 (May 2003).

9. All figures in this paragraph from Bunn, Holdren, and Weir, *Controlling Nuclear Warheads and Materials*, p. 80.

10. The Baker-Cutler estimates fail to account for the LEU produced after purchase of Russian HEU. The report recommends $11 billion to extend the current HEU purchase agreement to buy all excess Russian HEU, a goal we support. But while the current program is largely financed by the value of the power plant fuel produced from Russian HEU, the Baker-Cutler proposal never includes this source of revenue. Such a revenue source is likely to heavily reduce the cost of acquiring Russian HEU. If market concerns force the United States to sequester the LEU produced for roughly a decade, as is probable, the U.S. can deeply reduce its financing costs by blending down the Russian material to 19.9 percent LEU using significantly depleted blendstock.

11. Miles Pomper, "Bush Stresses Importance of Nunn-Lugar Programs but Cuts Funds in 2005 Budget Request," *Arms Control Today* 34 (March 2004).

12. For more on this topic, see Center for Strategic and International Studies (www.sgpproject.org [September 10, 2004]).

13. Carnegie Endowment for International Peace and Russian American Nuclear Security Advisory Council, *Reshaping U.S.-Russian Threat Reduction* (Washington: CEIP and RANSAC, 2002)

14. David Albright and Kevin O'Neill, eds., *The Challenges of Fissile Material Control* (Washington: Institute for Science and International Security Press, 1999).

15. Matthew Bunn, John P. Holdren, and Anthony Weir, *Securing Nuclear Weapons and Materials: Seven Steps for Immediate Action* (Harvard University, 2002); Robert J. Einhorn, ed., *Protecting against the Spread of Nuclear, Biological, and Chemical Weapons: An Action Agenda for the Global Partnership* (Washington: CSIS, 2003).

16. Bunn, Holdren, and Weir, *Securing Nuclear Weapons and Materials.*

17. Bunn, Holdren, and Weir, *Controlling Nuclear Warheads and Materials*, p. 156.

18. Ibid., p. 155.

19. U.S. Congress, *U.S. National Security and Military/Commercial Concerns with the People's Republic of China* (Government Printing Office, 1998).

20. *Treaty on the Non-Proliferation of Nuclear Weapons* (www.fas.org/nuke/control/npt/text/npt2.htm [September 8, 2004]).

21. For examples of this debate, see Council for a Livable World, "The U.S. and Pakistan: Allies, but no PALs," press release, October 31, 2001; David Albright, "Securing Pakistan's Nuclear Weapons Complex" (www.isis-online.org/publications/terrorism/stanleypaper.html [September 8, 2004]); Paolo Cotta-Ramusino and Maurizio Martellini, "Nuclear Safety, Nuclear Stability, and

Nuclear Strategy in Pakistan" (www.mi.infn.it/~landnet/Doc/pakistan.pdf [September 3, 2004]).

22. For more on information barriers, see, for example, D. A. Close, D. W. MacArthur, and N. J. Nicholas, "An Early Version of an Information Barrier," *Journal of Nuclear Materials Management* 31 (Fall 2002).

23. "Pakistan: Four Scenarios Considered for Nuclear Weapons Use," *Global Security Newswire*, February 4, 2002.

24. Conversation with Pervez Hoodbhoy, August 22, 2003.

25. Exchange with Richard Garwin, May 3, 2004.

26. Peter Feaver and Peter Stein, *Assuring Control of Nuclear Weapons: The Evolution of Permissive Action Links* (Lanham, Md.: University Press of America, 1987).

27. See, for example, Mansoor Ijaz and R. James Woolsey, "How Secure Is Pakistan's Plutonium?" *New York Times*, November 28, 2001; Jon Wolfsthal, "U.S. Needs a Contingency Plan for Pakistan's Nuclear Arsenal," *Los Angeles Times*, October 16, 2001.

28. For an extensive technical discussion, see Jay C. Davis, "The Attribution of WMD Events," *Journal of Homeland Security*, April 2003

29. National Academy of Sciences, *Making the Nation Safer* (Washington: National Academy Press, 2002).

30. Conversation with Ivan Oelrich, Federation of American Scientists.

31. See, for example, Non-Proliferation Policy Education Center, *Iran: Breaking Out without Quite Breaking the Rules?*(www.npec-web.org/pages/iranswu.htm [September 8, 2004]).

32. See World Information Service on Energy Uranium Project, "World Nuclear Fuel Facilities" (www.antenna.nl/wise/uranium/efac.html [September 13, 2004]). See also Institute for Energy and Environmental Research, *Energy and Security* 2 (January 1997) (www.ieer.org/ensec/no-2/repromap.html [September 3, 2004]).

33. Robert L. Civiak, *Closing the Gaps: Securing Highly Enriched Uranium in the Former Soviet Union and Eastern Europe* (Washington: Federation of American Scientists, 2002).

34. Two alternatives have been suggested, but neither is appropriate. CANDU reactors operate using natural uranium and thus do not require enrichment, but instead they produce plutonium highly suited to nuclear weapons. Some have suggested that we simply operate off downblended weapons-HEU, but even if all the world's weapons were converted to power plant fuel, it would last fewer than five years at current rates of nuclear power use.

35. John Deutch and others, *The Future of Nuclear Power* (Massachussetts Institute of Technology, 2003).

36. L. Scheinman, "Multinational Alternatives and Nuclear Nonproliferation," *International Organization* 35 (Winter 1981).

37. Deutch and others, *The Future of Nuclear Power.*

38. Charles Curtis has proposed a similar scheme, under which all new fuel-cycle facilities would have to be placed under IAEA custody. Though this could be similarly effective, it is highly doubtful that the United States would agree to such an arrangement for its fuel-cycle facilities. Multinational facilities could achieve the same ends without running the high risk of domestic political opposition to UN custodianship of American facilities.

39. See, for example, Matthew Bunn and others, *The Economics of Reprocessing vs. Direct Disposal of Spent Nuclear Fuel* (Harvard University, 2003); and Deutch and others, *The Future of Nuclear Power.*

40. Conversation with Edwin Lyman, August 2003.

41. David Albright, Frans Berkhout, and William Walker, *Plutonium and Highly Enriched Uranium, 1996: World Inventories, Capabilities and Policies* (Solna, Sweden: SIPRI, 1997).

42. George W. Bush, "Remarks by the President on Weapons of Mass Destruction Proliferation," February 11, 2001 (www.whitehouse.gov/news/releases/2004/02/20040211-4.html [September 8, 2004]).

43. For example, Mohamed ElBaradei, "Saving Ourselves from Self-Destruction," *New York Times*, February 12, 2004.

44. The discussion of INFCE in this paragraph is based on Joseph P. Nye, "Maintaining a Nonproliferation Regime," *International Organization* 35 (Winter 1981) and Philip Gummett, "From NPT to INFCE: Developments in Thinking about Nuclear Non-Proliferation," *International Affairs* 57 (Autumn 1981).

45. For an extensive discussion of both types of means of detection, from which this section draws in part, see *Nuclear Safeguards and the International Atomic Energy Agency* (U.S. Congress, Office of Technology Assessment, 1995).

46. Howard Diamond, "IAEA Approves '93+2' Protocol; Awaits Adoption by Member-States," *Arms Control Today* 27 (May 1997).

47. The discussion of whistle-blowers is drawn from Michael A. Levi, "Weapons Scientists as Whistle Blowers," *World Policy Journal* (Winter 2003).

48. United Nations, *Convention Relating to the Status of Refugees* (New York: 1951).

49. For discussion of a recent effort to do this, see "Iraq II: Bill Would Provide Safe U.S. Haven for Iraqi Scientists," *Global Security Newswire*, October 31, 2002.

50. Uranium enrichment plants combine large numbers of individual enrichment components into "cascades" that together can enrich uranium to higher grades.

51. Federation of American Scientists, "Nuclear Suppliers Group" (www.fas.org/nuke/control/nsg/index.html [September 3, 2004]).

52. General Accounting Office, "Nonproliferation: Strategy Needed to Strengthen Multilateral Export Control Regimes" (Government Printing Office, 2002).

53. Michael Beck and others, *Strengthening Multilateral Export Controls* (University of Georgia, 2002).

54. George Tenet, "Iraq and Weapons of Mass Destruction," speech given at Georgetown University, February 5, 2004 (www.cia.gov/cia/public_affairs/speeches/2004/tenet_georgetownspeech_02052004.html [September 8, 2004]).

55. David Albright and Corey Hinderstein, "Iran, Player or Rogue?" *Bulletin of the Atomic Scientists* 59 (September/October 2003).

56. General Accounting Office, "Nonproliferation: Strategy Needed to Strengthen Multilateral Export Control Regimes."

57. Beck and others, *Strengthening Multilateral Export Controls.*

58. Michael Levi, "Uncontainable: North Korea's Loose Nukes," *New Republic*, May 26, 2003.

59. Baker Spring, "Harnessing the Power of Nations for Arms Control: The Proliferation Security Initiative and Coalitions of the Willing," *Heritage Backgrounder* 1737 (March 2004).

60. Judith Miller, "Panama Joins Accord to Stem Ships' Transport of Illicit Arms," *New York Times*, May 11, 2004, p. A11.

61. This discussion draws on Michael Levi and Michael O'Hanlon, "A Global Solution Is Needed for Illicit Weapons," *Financial Times* (London), July 10, 2003.

62. Miller, "Panama Joins Accord."

63. Kurt M. Campbell, "Reconsidering a Nuclear Future: Why Countries Might Cross Over to the Other Side," in *The Nuclear Tipping Point: Why States Reconsider Their Nuclear Choices*, edited by Kurt M. Campbell, Robert J. Einhorn, and Mitchell B. Reiss (Washington: Brookings, 2004), pp. 28–29.

64. For a good analysis of some of the key states at issue, such as Egypt and Saudi Arabia, see Campbell, Einhorn, and Reiss, *The Nuclear Tipping Point.*

65. Ann Devroy, "Pact Reached to Dismantle Ukraine's Nuclear Force," *Washington Post*, January 10, 1994, p. A1; Letter from the Permanent Representatives of the Russian Federation, Ukraine, the United Kingdom, and the United States to the United Nations, December 19, 1994, document A/49/765 and S/1994/1399.

Chapter Four

1. For an overview, see Mark Wheelis, "Biotechnology and Biochemical Weapons," *Nonproliferation Review* (Spring 2002): 48–53.

2. For more on this, see Rebecca Katz, "Public Health Preparedness: The Best Defense against Biological Weapons," *Washington Quarterly* 25 (Summer 2002): 69–82.

3. Australian researchers have joined mousepox with the gene for interleukin-4. Carina Dennis, "The Bugs of War," *Nature* 411 (May 17, 2001): 232–35, available at www.nature.com.

4. Judith Miller, Stephen Engelberg, and William Broad, *Germs: Biological Weapons and America's Secret War* (New York: Simon and Schuster, 2001), pp. 232–33; Sheryl Gay Stolberg, "Some Experts Say U.S. Is Vulnerable to a Germ Attack," *New York Times*, September 30, 2001, p. A1; and John D. Steinbruner, "Biological Weapons: A Plague upon All Houses," *Foreign Policy* 109 (Winter 1997–98): 88.

5. Steven M. Block, "The Growing Threat of Biological Weapons," *American Scientist Online*, January/February 2001, p. 9 (www.americanscientist.org [September 3, 2004]).

6. See Committee on Research Standards and Practices to Prevent the Destructive Application of Biotechnology, *Biotechnology Research in an Age of Terrorism: Confronting the Dual Use Dilemma* (Washington.: National Research Council of the National Academy of Sciences, 2003).

7. John D. Steinbruner and Elisa D. Harris, "Controlling Dangerous Pathogens," *Issues in Science and Technology* (Spring 2003), p. 52.

8. Raymond A. Zilinskas and Jonathan B. Tucker, "Limiting the Contribution of the Open Scientific Literature to the Biological Weapons Threat," Report of the Workshop on Guidelines for the Publication of Scientific Research Potentially Related to Biological and Toxin Warfare, Washington, D.C., August 12, 2002.

9. Block, "The Growing Threat of Biological Weapons," p. 7.

10. On the former Soviet states, see Kenneth N. Luongo and others, "Securing Former Soviet Biological Weapons," *Arms Control Today* 34, no. 6 (July–August 2004): 18–23.

11. Mark Wheelis and Malcolm Dando, "Back to Bioweapons?" *Bulletin of the Atomic Scientists* (January/February 2003): 40–46; and Barbara Hatch Rosenberg, "Defending against Biodefence: The Need for Limits," *Disarmament Diplomacy* (February/March 2003): 1–6.

12. Daryl Kimball and Kerry Boyd, "Briefing Paper on the Status of Biological Weapons Nonproliferation," Arms Control Association, Washington, May 2003 (www.armscontrol.org/factsheets/bwissuebrief.asp?print [September 7, 2004]).

13. U.S. Department of State, "Decision of the Fifth Review Conference of the States Parties to the Convention on the Prohibition of the Development, Production, and Stockpiling of Bacteriological (Biological) Weapons and on Their Destruction," Washington, December 12, 2002 (www.state.gov/t/ac/rls/or/2002/15725pf.htm [September 7, 2004]).

14. Miller, Engelberg, and Broad, *Germs*, pp. 287–310.

15. Under Secretary of State John Bolton, "The U.S. Position on the Biological Weapons Convention: Combating the BW Threat," Tokyo, Japan, August 26, 2002 (www.state.gov/t/us/rm/13090pf.htm [September 7, 2004]).

16. Article 14.6 reads that state parties should "(a) Not establish, maintain or take either individually or collectively any discriminatory measures, including those in any international agreements incompatible with the obligations

undertaken in the Convention, which would hamper the economic and technological development of States Parties to the Convention or international cooperation in the field of peaceful bacteriological (biological) activities in accordance with the provisions of the Convention, including research in biology, microbiology, biotechnology and genetic engineering, and their industrial, agricultural, medical and pharmaceutical applications; and other related areas for peaceful purposes."

17. Jonathan B. Tucker, "U.S. Biosecurity Legislation," *Arms Control Today* 33 (June 2003): 5.

18. Jonathan B. Tucker, "Preventing the Misuse of Pathogens: The Need for Global Biosecurity Standards," *Arms Control Today* 33 (June 2003): 5–7.

19. For an example of this type of idea, see Michael Barletta, Amy Sands, and Jonathan B. Tucker, "Keeping Track of Anthrax: The Case for a Biosecurity Convention," *Bulletin of the Atomic Scientists* (May/June 2002): 61–62.

20. Michael Beck and Seema Gahlaut, "Creating a New Multilateral Export Control Regime," *Arms Control Today* 33 (April 2003): 12–18.

21. Tucker, "Preventing the Misuse of Pathogens," p. 8.

22. Steinbruner and Harris, "Controlling Dangerous Pathogens," pp. 47–54.

23. Christopher F. Chyba and Alex L. Greninger, "Biotechnology and Bioterrorism: An Unprecedented World," *Survival* 46 (Summer 2004): 143–62.

24. Christopher F. Chyba, "Toward Biological Security," *Foreign Affairs* 81 (May/June 2002): 136; and Dennis, "The Bugs of War," pp. 234–35.

25. Scott D. Sagan, "The Commitment Trap: Why the United States Should Not Use Nuclear Threats to Deter Biological and Chemical Weapons Attacks," *International Security* 24 (Spring 2000): 85–115; and Steve Fetter, "Limiting the Role of Nuclear Weapons," in *The Nuclear Turning Point*, edited by Harold A. Feiveson (Brookings, 1999), pp. 35–41.

26. See Richard Butler, *The Greatest Threat* (New York: Public Affairs, 2000); and Hans Blix, *Disarming Iraq* (New York: Pantheon Books, 2004).

27. See Bill Joy, "Why the Future Doesn't Need Us," *Wired*, April 2000.

28. On the latter view, see Freeman J. Dyson, "The Future Needs Us!" *New York Review of Books*, February 13, 2003.

29. Robert Park, "Tiny Terrors," *New Scientist*, July 5, 2003, p. 22.

30. Richard E. Smalley, "Of Chemistry, Love, and Nanobots," *Scientific American*, September 2001, pp. 76–77.

31. See Sean Howard, "Nanotechnology and Mass Destruction: The Need for an Inner Space Treaty," *Disarmament Diplomacy* (July/August 2002).

32. Congress is showing some interest in mandating such studies; see David Malakoff, "Congress Wants Studies of Nanotech's 'Dark Side,'" *Science* 301 (July 4, 2003), p. 27. The United Kingdom's Royal Society and the Royal Academy of Engineering have just conducted such a study; see Fiona Profitt, "Yellow Light for Nanotech," *Science* 305 (August 6, 2004), p. 762.

33. National Academy of Sciences, *Cybersecurity Today and Tomorrow* (Washington: National Academy of Sciences, 2003), p. 6.

34. Arnaud de Borchgrave and others, "Cyber Threats and Information Security: Meeting the 21st Century Challenge" (Washington: Center for Strategic and International Studies, December 2000).

35. The General Accounting Office has documented numerous security flaws in government computer systems. See, for example, General Accounting Office, "Information Security: Serious and Widespread Weaknesses Persist at Federal Agencies," GAO/AIMD-00-295, September 2000.

36. Renae Merle, "IT Groups Says Security Is Underfunded," *Washington Post*, February 1, 2002, page E5.

37. The Office of Personnel Management recently put forward a proposal to create a new Senior Civil Service, comprising two corps: the Senior Executive Corps (SEC) and the Senior Professional Corps (SPC). The purpose of the reform would be to provide the same level of prestige and attractiveness to the two corps, thus eliminating the current discrepancy between the Senior Executive Service and SL/ST positions; under the new plan, senior government officials who are truly fulfilling executive functions would enter the SEC, whereas senior technical experts would enter the SPC. Increasing the attractiveness of the civil service for technical workers—which a reform like this would help to accomplish—could help to induce highly skilled computer programmers to join the government.

38. Richard K. Betts, "Fixing Intelligence," *Foreign Affairs* (January/February 2002).

39. National Research Council, *Cybersecurity Today and Tomorrow: Pay Now or Pay Later* (Washington: National Academy of Sciences, 2002), pp. 13–15.

40. Ibid., p. 9.

41. For more background on this general issue, see President's Commission on Critical Infrastructure Protection, *Critical Foundations: Protecting America's Infrastructures* (1997); Bill Gertz, "Pentagon Fortifying Computer Networks to Stymie Hackers," *Washington Times*, April 17, 1998, p. A3; Glenn Buchan, "Implications of Information Vulnerabilities for Military Operations," in *The Changing Role of Information in Warfare*, edited by Zalmay Khalilzad, A. H. Marshall, and John P. White (Santa Monica, Calif.: RAND, 1999), pp. 290–95; and Gloria Wilt, "Making Information Safe," *Science and Technology Review*, Lawrence Livermore National Laboratory (January/February 1998), pp. 4–11.

Chapter Five

1. Anne-Marie Slaughter, "A Chance to Reshape the U.N.," *Washington Post*, April 13, 2003.

2. Lee Feinstein and Anne-Marie Slaughter, "A Duty to Prevent," *Foreign Affairs* 83 (January/February 2004).

3. Ibid.

4. For a shorter list focused on stopping states without internal checks on their power from proliferating, see Feinstein and Slaughter, "A Duty to Prevent," pp. 136–50.

5. *The National Security Strategy of the United States of America* (White House, 2002).

6. Colin L. Powell, "A Strategy of Partnerships," *Foreign Affairs* 83 (January/February 2004), p. 24.

7. For more, see Michael O'Hanlon and Mike Mochizuki, *Crisis on the Korean Peninsula: How to Deal with a Nuclear North Korea* (New York: McGraw-Hill, 2003).

8. For a similar view, see the speech by William J. Perry at the Brookings Institution, "Crisis on the Korean Peninsula: Implications for U.S. Policy in Northeast Asia," Washington, January 24, 2003 (www.brookings.edu).

9. See Doug Struck, "Citing Iraq, N. Korea Signals Hard Line on Weapons Issues," *Washington Post*, March 30, 2003, p. 30; and James Brooke, "North Korea Watches War and Wonders What's Next," *New York Times*, March 31, 2003.

10. For a similar view, see Gary Samore, "The Korean Nuclear Crisis," *Survival* 45 (Spring 2003), pp. 19–22.

11. Central Intelligence Agency, "Unclassified Report to Congress on the Acquisition of Technology Relating to Weapons of Mass Destruction and Advanced Conventional Munitions, 1 January through 30 June 2002" (www.cia.gov/cia/reports/721_reports/jan_jun2002.html#7 [September 3, 2004]).

12. Douglas Frantz, "Black Market Nuclear Probe Focuses on Syria," *Los Angeles Times*, June 24, 2004.

13. John R. Bolton, testimony before the Middle East and Central Asia Subcommittee of the House International Relations Committee, *Syria: Implications for U.S. Security and Regional Stability*, September 16, 2003.

14. John R. Bolton, "Beyond the Axis of Evil: Additional Threats from Weapons of Mass Destruction," *Heritage Lectures*, no. 743 (Washington: Heritage Foundation).

15. See Strobe Talbott, *Engaging India: Diplomacy, Democracy, and the Bomb* (Brookings, 2004), pp. 227–32.

16. For how such an effort should be conducted, see ibid., pp. 227–32.

Chapter Six

1. See Carnegie Commission on Preventing Deadly Conflict, *Preventing Deadly Conflict: Final Report* (New York: Carnegie Corporation, 1997), pp. 11–19; Yahya Sadowski, *The Myth of Global Chaos* (Brookings, 1998), pp. 130–40; and Ted Robert Gurr, Monty G. Marshall, and Deepa Khosla, *Peace*

and Conflict 2001 (College Park, Md.: Center for International Development and Conflict Management, 2001), pp. 7–9.

2. See Francis M. Deng and others, *Sovereignty as Responsibility: Conflict Management in Africa* (Brookings, 1996).

3. Philip Shenon, "U.S. Reaches Deal to Limit Transfers of Portable Missiles," *New York Times*, October 21, 2003, p. A1.

4. William Hartung and Rachel Stohl, "Hired Guns," *Foreign Policy* (May/June 2004): 28–29.

5. Nicholas Marsh, "Two Sides of the Same Coin? The Legal and Illegal Trade in Small Arms," *Brown Journal of World Affairs* 9 (Spring 2002): 217–20.

6. Jo L. Husbands, "The Proliferation of Conventional Weapons and Technologies," in *Grave New World*, edited by Michael E. Brown (Georgetown University Press, 2003), p. 69.

7. See Bjorn Hagelin and others, "International Arms Transfers," *SIPRI Yearbook 2003* (Oxford University Press, 2003), p. 439; and Richard F. Grimmett, *Conventional Arms Transfers to Developing Nations, 1994–2001* (Washington: Congressional Research Service, 2002), pp. 1–14.

8. For example, in 2002 arms deliveries to the developing world were led by the United States ($10.2 billion), United Kingdom ($4.7 billion), Russia ($3.1 billion), France ($1.8 billion), China ($800 million), Ukraine ($600 million), and Germany ($500 million), with Italy, Israel, Brazil, and Spain next on the list. New sales agreements included most of the same countries but in a different order, with Ukraine, Italy, and Germany among the top five and with France sixth, the United Kingdom ninth, and China eleventh. See Grimmett, *Conventional Arms Transfers to Developing Nations, 1995–2002* (Washington: Congressional Research Service, 2003), pp. 76, 81.

9. See, for example, Edward J. Laurance, *Light Weapons and Intrastate Conflict* (New York: Carnegie Corporation, 1998), p. 24; and Maria Haug and others, *Shining a Light on Small Arms Exports: The Record of State Transparency*, Occasional Paper No. 4, Norwegian Initiative on Small Arms Transfers (Oslo: January 2002), p. 3, available at www.nisat.org.

10. Joanna Spear, "Disarmament and Demobilization," in *Ending Civil Wars: The Implementation of Peace Agreements*, edited by Stephen John Stedman, Donald Rothchild, and Elizabeth M. Cousens (London: Lynne Rienner Publishers, 2002), pp. 156–58.

11. Robert W. Sherman, "The Real Terrorist Missile Threat, and What Can Be Done about It," *Public Interest Report* 56 (Washington: Federation of American Scientists), 2003.

12. Husbands, "The Proliferation of Conventional Weapons and Technologies," p. 76.

13. See Lora Lumpe and Jeff Donarski, *The Arms Trade Revealed* (Washington: Federation of American Scientists, 1998), pp. 2–3.

14. International Committee of the Red Cross, "Meeting of States on the Illicit Trade in Small Arms and Light Weapons," July 2003, available at www.icrc.org/Web/Eng.

15. Council of European Union, "EU Programme for Preventing and Combating Illicit Trafficking in Conventional Arms," 1996, available at www.fas.org/asmp/campaigns/smallarms/euprogram.htm; and Center for Defense Information, "United States Weakens Outcome of UN Small Arms and Light Weapons Conference," September 2002 (www.cdi.org/friendlyversion/printversion.cfm?documentID=629&from_page=../pro [September 7, 2004]).

16. Marsh, "Two Sides of the Same Coin?" pp. 218–19.

17. Haug and others, *Shining a Light on Small Arms Exports: The Record of State Transparency*, p. 16.

18. Lora Lumpe, "A 'New' Approach to the Small Arms Trade," *Arms Control Today* 31 (January/February 2001), pp. 11–17.

19. Agence France-Presse, "'Blood Diamonds' Process Gives Laggard Countries Another Month," July 31, 2003; Global Witness Press Release, "Kimberley Process Finally Agrees Membership List but Lack of Monitoring Undermines Credibility," July 31, 2003 (www.globalwitness.org/press_ releases/display2.php?id=214 [September 7, 2004]).

20. Global Witness, "The Logs of War: The Timber Trade and Armed Conflict," 2002, available at www.globalwitness.org/reports/ [September 8, 2004]).

21. Physicians for Human Rights, *Landmines: A Deadly Legacy* (New York: Human Rights Watch, 2003), pp. 3–15.

22. See Michael Flynn, "Political Minefield," *Bulletin of the Atomic Scientists* 55 (March/April 1999); and Richard Price, "Reversing the Gun Sights: Transnational Civil Society Targets Land Mines," *International Organization* 52 (Summer 1998): 613–44.

23. Caleb Rossiter, *Winning in Korea without Landmines*, Vietnam Veterans of America Foundation Monograph Series 1 (Summer 2000), pp. 29–31.

24. Japanese Ministry of Foreign Affairs, *Japan's Disarmament Policy* (Tokyo: Japan Institute of International Affairs, 2003), p. 92.

25. Wade Boese, "U.S. Might Use Landmines in Iraq; Future Policy Unclear," *Arms Control Today* 33 (April 2003): 26; and Wade Boese, "U.S. Military Did Not Use Landmines in Iraq War," *Arms Control Today* 33 (July/August 2003): 30.

26. International Institute for Strategic Studies, *The Military Balance 2002–2003* (Oxford University Press, 2002), pp. 145–48 and 163–65.

27. See Robert L. Suettinger, *Beyond Tiananmen* (Brookings, 2003), pp. 200–63.

28. On China's economy, see Nicholas R. Lardy, *China's Unfinished Economic Revolution* (Brookings, 1998); on its rise, see Ashton B. Carter and William J. Perry, *Preventive Defense* (Brookings, 1999), pp. 92–122.

29. Among the most illuminating recent writings on China's foreign policy and military capabilities are Scott Kennedy, ed., *China Cross Talk* (New York: Rowman and Littlefield Publishers, 2003); Thomas J. Christensen, "Posing Problems without Catching Up: China's Rise and Challenges for U.S. Security Policy," *International Security* 25 (Spring 2001): 5–40; Larry M. Wortzel, *The Chinese Armed Forces in the 21st Century* (Carlisle, Pa.: Strategic Studies Institute, 1999); and James R. Lilley and Chuck Downs, *Crisis in the Taiwan Strait* (Washington: National Defense University, 1997).

30. John J. Tkacik Jr., "Washington Must Head Off European Arms Sales to China," *Heritage Backgrounder* 1739 (March 2004).

31. International Institute for Strategic Studies, *The Military Balance 2002–2003*, pp. 129–35.

32. For a good overview, see Stephen P. Cohen, *India: Emerging Power* (Brookings, 2001), pp. 127–227.

33. Ranked by defense spending, the regional powers appear in this order: Saudi Arabia, Israel, Kuwait, Iran, Egypt, Syria, United Arab Emirates, Oman, Syria, and Iraq. Ranked by the size of forces and equipment inventories, however, the first tier is composed of Iran, Iraq, Syria, Egypt, and Israel, with the Gulf states all well behind by most numerical measures. International Institute for Strategic Studies, *The Military Balance 2002–2003*, pp. 101–21, 333. On Syria, see Geoffrey Kemp, *The Control of the Middle East Arms Race* (Washington: Carnegie Endowment, 1991), pp. 3–6.

34. For a similar argument about a different region, see Richard K. Betts, "Systems for Peace or Causes of War? Collective Security, Arms Control, and the New Europe," *International Security* 17, no. 1 (Summer 1992): 5–43.

35. See Joshua M. Epstein, "Dynamic Analysis and the Conventional Balance in Europe," *International Security* 12 (Spring 1988): 154–65; and Richard K. Betts, *Surprise Attack* (Brookings, 1982), pp. 3–149.

36. See Michael Krepon, "Nuclear Risk Reduction: Is Cold War Experience Applicable to Southern Asia?" (Washington: Stimson Center, June 2001), available at www.stimson.org; and Peter R. Lavoy, "South Asia," in *Arms Control: Cooperative Security in a Changing Environment*, edited by Jeffrey A. Larsen (Boulder, Co.: Lynne Rienner Publishers, 2002), pp. 241–52.

37. For the sensitivities associated with any such tightening of U.S.-Taiwan ties, see Michael D. Swaine, *Taiwan's National Security, Defense Policy, and Weapons Procurement Processes* (Santa Monica, Calif.: RAND, 1999), pp. 73–76.

38. Walter B. Slocombe and others, *Missile Defense in Asia*, Policy Paper (Washington: Atlantic Council, 2003), p. x.

39. See Kenneth M. Pollack, "Securing the Gulf," *Foreign Affairs* 82 (July/August 2003): 13.

40. See Michael O'Hanlon, Victoria Farrell, and Steven Glazerman, *Limiting Conventional Arms Exports to the Middle East* (Washington: Congressional Budget Office, 1992).

41. For an earlier argument that remains relevant in many ways, see Geoffrey Kemp, *The Control of the Middle East Arms Race* (Washington: Carnegie Endowment, 1991), pp. 177–83.

42. See O'Hanlon, Farrell, and Glazerman, *Limiting Conventional Arms Exports to the Middle East.*

43. For a similar argument, see Michael O'Hanlon and Mike Mochizuki, *Crisis on the Korean Peninsula: Dealing with a Nuclear North Korea* (New York: McGraw-Hill, 2003).

44. For a similar argument, see Seo-Hang Lee, "Arms Control on the Korean Peninsula: Background and Issues," in *The Korean Peninsula and Korea-U.S. Relations* (Seoul: Institute of Foreign Affairs and National Security, 1997), pp. 3–13.

45. See CSIS Working Group, *Conventional Arms Control on the Korean Peninsula* (Washington: Center for Strategic and International Studies, August 2002), pp. 13–17; and Lee, "Arms Control on the Korean Peninsula," p. 11.

46. For an analysis of some of the main elements of the CFE Treaty and prior negotiations, see Frances M. Lussier, "Budgetary and Military Effects of a Treaty Limiting Conventional Forces in Europe," CBO Paper, Congressional Budget Office, September 1990, pp. 25–39.

47. Much of this is based on Pedro Almeida and Michael O'Hanlon, "Impasse in Korea: A Conventional Arms Accord Solution?" *Survival* 41 (Spring 1999), pp. 58–72.

Index

THE BROOKINGS INSTITUTION

The Brookings Institution is an independent organization devoted to nonpartisan research, education, and publication in economics, government, foreign policy, and the social sciences generally. Its principal purposes are to aid in the development of sound public policies and to promote public understanding of issues of national importance. The Institution was founded on December 8, 1927, to merge the activities of the Institute for Government Research, founded in 1916, the Institute of Economics, founded in 1922, and the Robert Brookings Graduate School of Economics and Government, founded in 1924. The Institution maintains a position of neutrality on issues of public policy to safeguard the intellectual freedom of the staff. Interpretations or conclusions in Brookings publications should be understood to be solely those of the authors.